The Truth About
Middle Managers

The Truth About Middle Managers

Who They Are, How They Work, Why They Matter

Paul Osterman

Harvard Business Press

Boston, Massachusetts

Printed in the United States of America
12 11 10 09 08   5 4 3 2 1

Library of Congress Cataloging-in-Publication Data

Osterman, Paul.
    The truth about middle managers: who they are, how they work,
why they matter / Paul Osterman.
        p. cm.
    Includes index.
    ISBN 978-1-4221-7970-3
    1. Middle managers.   2. Management.   I. Title.
    HD38.24.O88 2008
    658.4'3—dc22

                                                        2008026780

The paper used in this publication meets the requirements of the American
National Standard for Permanence of Paper for Publications and Documents
in Libraries and Archives Z39.48-1992.

CONTENTS

PREFACE AND
ACKNOWLEDGMENTS

This book was born out of my reflections about the constant turmoil and uncertainty inside organizations. In previous research, I wrote about the impact of these upheavals on frontline workers. In some respects, frontline people suffered as they lost jobs and found themselves in an increasingly uncertain environment, but in other ways, they benefited as work became broader and more challenging.

Because middle managers are at the center of restructuring, I began to think about their fate. I realized that our understanding of the changes affecting this group is confused. Everyone seemed to agree that the world of the Organization Man is over, but what is replacing it? Middle managers are just like ordinary workers in that neither group makes the big decisions that drive restructuring. Both groups are acted on rather than acting. But unlike other employees, middle managers are presumed to identify with the firm and its goals and have historically been protected from economic turbulence. Daily headlines proclaim that this protection has ended and for many people this is clearly bad news. However, perhaps surprisingly, some observers view the change as a form of liberation. They celebrate "intrapreneurs" and other forms of "boundaryless careers." What's more, with the reduction of managerial layers, the people who remained might find themselves exercising more discretion and enjoying broader work. On the other hand, they might also find themselves under much more pressure than in the past. And how have managers reacted? Do they still identify with their employers, or has their commitment attenuated? To what are they loyal?

My first step in sorting out this confusion was some open-ended interviews. Ruthanne Huising, a graduate student at Sloan, joined me in these and later conducted some interviews on her own. Her reactions and thoughts were always insightful and stimulating. As I began to think through the shape of the book, Joe Rosenblom was helpful with his useful, and frequently skeptical, feedback. Diane Burton has thought deeply about the questions that drive this book; my conversations with her were always enlightening.

Several colleagues took the time to read the draft manuscript, and they each provided helpful comments. I thank Peter Cappelli, Thomas Kochan, Robert McKersie, and Michael Useem.

I was fortunate to have Melinda Merino and Brian Surette as editors. They were both skillful and persistent, and the book is much better for their efforts. The editorial production staff at the Press did a wonderful job.

My wife, Susan Eckstein, read portions of the book and gave me useful feedback. She also put up with a great deal of moaning and groaning and helped push me to the conclusion.

The Truth About
Middle Managers

Introduction

What's Happened to
Middle Managers?

Management and managers are
a source of endless fascination and analysis, but the attention
managers get is skewed. Nearly all writing, popular and scholarly, centers on CEOs and the pretenders to that title.[1] They are
exalted for their achievements (Jack Welch of General Electric)
or attacked for their failures (Charles Prince of Citicorp). More
serious research examines how they make decisions, what their
work consists of, and how they got to be where they are. But
there are far fewer managers at the top than there are in the
middle, and taken as a group, middle managers have as much to

say about organizational success or failure as do those at the top. Yet our understanding of middle management is remarkably thin, compared with research conducted on higher management.

There are multiple puzzles about middle management. Take, for example, the impact of restructuring on middle managers' careers and jobs. One view is that middle managers have been as much the victims of restructuring as have blue-collar employees. Managers are seen as wasteful overhead. Corporate raider Carl Icahn described his strategy for making money as eliminating "layers of bureaucrats reporting to bureaucrats."[2] Popular management guru Tom Peters is similarly disparaging: "Am I a middle management basher? Yes. Are most of the people who attend my seminars middle managers? Yes. Why do they come? Beats me."[3] Other experts pile on. Peter Drucker declared that "middle managements today tend to be overstaffed to the point of obesity," and Jack Welch observed that "we were hiring people just to read the reports of people who had been hired to write reports."[4]

There are, however, alternative views. One version simply points out that organizations are a pervasive feature of modern life. Although it may be fun to mock bureaucracy, the argument goes, without efficient organizations, we would lack the products and services that we have come to expect and that are responsible for modern living standards. Managers make organizations run. Another viewpoint actually sees managers as beneficiaries of the newly restructured organizations. Instead of being trapped in stultifying bureaucracies, middle managers are now free to be "intrapreneurs," to take charge of their own careers, and, like many other professionals, to enjoy the benefits of mobility and portable skills.

Other important questions about middle managers remain unanswered. How has their work changed? What is important to them in their work? How do they think about their circumstances, and what impact has managers' experience had on their loyalty to their employer and to corporate America? Are there political dimensions or consequences to their experience?

Why should we care? Today, 8 percent of the workforce is classified by the U.S. Census as managers. Using a more realistic definition, research shows that 19 percent of employees wear white collars and report that supervising others is a major part of their job.[5] The circumstances of these managers have long been at the heart of how both social science and literature think about a society composed of large organizations. More practically, the performance of those organizations depends largely on the commitment, skill, and effort of managers. In addition, there are significant parallels between the fate that has befallen middle managers and what has happened to other professionals. Doctors find themselves working in large bureaucracies, with all the constraints and opportunities that this entails. More and more professors are "adjuncts," without the kind of employment security that was once taken for granted in their profession. It is a rare scientist who can work in splendid isolation in the laboratory, free from the commercial and organizational demands of an employer. For better or worse, what is happening to managers is happening to many others as organizations restructure and respond to the new realities that they face.

ANSWERING THE QUESTIONS

The purpose of this book is to understand what has happened to middle managers as firms restructure. To this end, I conducted research on two firms in the Boston area: Fleet Bank, just as it was being acquired by Bank of America, and a high-tech firm I'll call TechCo. I interviewed fifty middle managers in 2004 and 2005 in the two firms, and I conducted multiple interviews of twelve of these interviewees several months apart. All interviews were taped and transcribed. The middle managers were chosen randomly from a list provided by the human resource staff in each organization. In addition, I interviewed another ten middle managers in Dallas. These managers were members of several large organizations that had self-help groups for laid-off members.

The interviews provide powerful and compelling portraits of middle managers. However, it is also important to work with more nationally representative data. To do this, I analyzed U.S. Census data from several years and a smaller but more in-depth national survey of managers. The survey, which was repeated over several decades, asked about working conditions and responsibilities. When I first turn to these data, I will provide, in the text and endnotes, a complete description of the surveys and how I used them.

WHO ARE MIDDLE MANAGERS?

No one has a job title "middle manager," and people do not come with labels. Who then are middle managers, and how do we distinguish them from those at the top? In my interviews,

I developed an operational definition by speaking either with people who were not individual producers but who led a team or with people who managed a set of team leaders. All these managers were salaried, had at least a college degree and very often more, and were on a managerial track. But beyond the practical research definition, it would also be useful to have a more abstract idea in mind.

When the sociologist C. Wright Mills did his pioneering work in the 1950s on the rise of white-collar workers, he described middle managers in disparaging terms: "You are the cog and the beltline of the bureaucratic machinery itself . . . and such power as you wield is a borrowed thing. Yours is the subordinate's mark, yours is the canned talk . . . you are the servant of decision, the assistant of authority."[6] This comment is suffused with a contempt that is both unfair and inaccurate, but it does nonetheless identify the key dividing line between the middle and the top. Senior management makes the decisions that set the organization's course, whereas middle management interprets and executes those decisions.

Management scholar John Kotter systematically examined the work of top managers and identified "agenda setting" as their key activity. Middle managers do not set agendas, but carry them out. Nonetheless, middle managers make numerous decisions, and these decisions are important to the organization. The context of these decisions, however, is not of the managers' own making. Put differently, the common fate of middle managers is that the nature of their careers and the character of their working life are largely outside their control. Middle managers live inside organizations and have little voice regarding the strategies of those organizations. In this sense, they differ from both the managers on top of the organizations and even from the front-line workers, who are usually represented by unions.

Top managers set the organization's strategy: what markets to enter, with whom to merge, how much to invest, what technology to employ. Their world is also buffeted by powerful forces over which they have modest control, but nonetheless their decisions are somewhat autonomous and shape the trajectory of their firms. The power of senior management to shape the path of its organizations is demonstrated by recent research that tracked top managers as they moved from one firm to another.[7] The researchers found that these managers carried with them personal approaches toward both financial and organizational decisions. By observing a firm's financial strategy, one can tell that it was CEO A who had made this decision, whereas at another firm, which followed a different strategy, it was CEO B. Even more interestingly, the authors found that personal style mattered the most in decisions regarding acquisitions and cost-cutting, just the kind of decisions most likely to affect the (helpless) middle managers.

Frontline workers represented by unions do not share the catbird seat with top management. As any student of the airline or automobile industry can attest, unions have been pummeled by competition, deregulation, and globalization. Nonetheless, just how the firms respond to these pressures is, in no small part, the consequence of union strategies and tactics. As an example, the United Automobile Workers may choose from many dimensions to provide some relief to employers: higher health-care deductibles, wage cuts, work rules that are more flexible, early retirements, acquiescence in plant closings. The choices and trade-offs that the union makes have significant consequences both for the firms and for their employees.

None of this is true for middle managers. In the movie *The Gods Must Be Crazy*, a Coke bottle thrown from a plane lands on the ground in the Kalahari Desert, and the Bushmen recipients, who have had no contact with the rest of the world, struggle to make sense of this message. The middle managers' circumstance bears an uncomfortable resemblance to this story.

ASSESSING SOME COMMON ASSUMPTIONS ABOUT MIDDLE MANAGERS

Because so much of the management literature emphasizes senior management, our understanding of the circumstances of middle management is based on media impressions and assumptions. Our understanding also draws from a rather elegiac social science literature of which Mills is representative. As a result, knowledge of middle management has endured a series of myths or misunderstandings, which this book aims to set straight.

- *Because of restructuring, the ranks of middle management have been greatly reduced and job security is nonexistent.* This is only partly true, and a paradox lurks in the data. Managerial work is no doubt less secure, and the interviews show that stress levels have gone up sharply. Insecurity is reflected in the decrease in the average time that managers spend with an employer (job tenure). But despite this trend, there has been a steady increase in the

number of employees who are managers. This increase
holds, even after it is controlled for the changing industrial distribution of the economy. In short, middle managers are less secure, but more in demand.

- *Middle managers are empire builders who do little useful
  work for their organizations.* The reality, as is clear from
  the interviews I conducted, is that middle managers are
  the glue that hold organizations together. They perform
  specific tasks themselves and they lead groups that make
  the products and that do the work of the organization.
  Middle managers are also ambassadors between top management and the workforce and between the many teams
  that make organizations function.

- *The work of middle management has been de-skilled by
  restructuring.* The reality is that work has changed along
  two dimensions: control and breadth. Because information technology enables better monitoring and organizations are flatter, middle managers are indeed more subject
  to the control of top executives than in the past. However,
  the same flattening of organizations means that the work
  of middle managers, their range of tasks and responsibilities, is broader (and more interesting) than in the
  past.

- *Because of layoffs and because top management seems to be
  protecting itself, middle managers have lost their sense of
  loyalty to their employers.* This observation is accurate.
  My interviews dramatically demonstrate this negative

attitudinal shift, which the middle managers directly attribute to what they see as top management's deception and greed. This sense of distance is intensified by organizational changes that make it harder for middle managers to climb the corporate ladder. These attitudes show up in my interviews and in a survey I conducted with young recent MBA graduates. The young respondents express a remarkable degree of cynicism regarding their employers. At the same time (and surprisingly, given their strongly critical assessment of their employers), my survey of the political attitudes of middle managers reveals that they draw no negative general conclusions, either economic or political, about how business operates. They believe that layoffs and restructuring are a normal and justified part of capitalism.

• *Because of this loss of loyalty, middle managers are alienated from their work and have little commitment to what they do.* This is emphatically not true. Middle managers very much enjoy what they do and have what I term a strong craft commitment to their work. Ironically, at the same time that they have lost their loyalty to their firm, their attachment to what they do and their desire to execute it well is strong and consistent.

Taken as a whole, these patterns lead to a final conclusion about the mind-set of middle managers. They live in a small world. Although they are committed to their jobs and their immediate colleagues and subordinates, middle managers are alienated from their own organizations and ask few questions about the larger system in which they are embedded. They tend their own garden and do little more.

TWO MIDDLE MANAGERS' EXPERIENCE OF RESTRUCTURING

The findings outlined above imply a complex and textured portrait of middle managers. In the course of this book, my interviews will help flesh out in greater depth the nature of what has happened. We can get an early impression of the complexities by considering two examples.

Some managers do experience the layoffs and job loss that dominate most reports, and "Burton" is representative of this group.[8]

Burton had worked with Johnson Wax for thirty-two years. This Racine, Wisconsin–based firm had long been family owned and was known for its benevolent employment practices. Like so many others, it was taken over by outsiders. Toward the end of his tenure, Burton was a sales manager responsible for all territories west of the Mississippi. His wife also worked for Johnson, as had his father, who after a thirty-three-year career retired at sixty-five. As Burton tells the story, one day his new boss called him in and said, "Well, you just don't fit the profile of what we're looking for to move ahead, so we're going to let you retire." Burton reports replying, "Let me see, we're about a $275 million division, and in the last six months, I've brought you about $50 million worth of new business opportunity. What part of that doesn't fit with the profile?"

Burton explored filing an age discrimination lawsuit, but his lawyer advised him to take his buyout and get on with his life.

This was hard: "I guess everybody deals with it a little differently, but in my personal situation, first I had to deal with the initial pain, the initial loss . . . I mean, I'd never been fired from anything. I mean, yeah, I was able to retire, but I was fired." He then fell from grace. After a period of joblessness, he worked for a small janitorial supply firm that went bankrupt and then a larger manufacturer that ended up being bought out and laying off employees, Burton included. When I met him, he was unemployed again. His conclusion from all this? "Well, as it turns out, in today's day and age, I don't believe there's a company left that you're not more than a number."

Experiences like Burton's are wrenching. But these stories are not typical of circumstances of managers, the vast majority of whom keep their jobs. More typical is what happened to a manager whom I interviewed at Bank of America.

In 2004, Bank of America announced that it was acquiring Fleet Bank. Fleet itself was the product of mergers, the most recent and largest being its takeover of Bank of Boston. But Fleet, which had always been the wolf, suddenly found itself acting the sheep. Although Bank of America promised that overall New England employment levels would not be reduced, everyone knew that even if this promise were kept, a considerable amount of reshuffling was in order. And everyone also knew who would be calling the tune.

One of the managers affected by these events is "Nancy," a lending manager at Fleet. A divorced women in her midforties with one grown child, Nancy has an MBA from one of the top business schools. She supervised a team of a dozen bankers who served a segment of small and medium enterprises, and she loved her work. What was particularly appealing was interacting with her clients: "You're considered an insider in a lot of things, so you can have quite a close relationship with the companies you deal with. I love the stories. I have a great respect for entrepreneurs."

Although very committed to her job and to her team, Nancy was no fan of the rituals of corporate culture and was far from the Organization Man ("I don't like corporate. I don't like regimentation. I don't like the group thing"). When I first met her, she had no cell phone and refused to do any e-mail from home in the evenings or on weekends. She had an intense private life— sports and a vacation home, to which she retreated on weekends—and was unwilling to let Fleet interfere. As a reward for good work, she had recently been invited to a corporate retreat in a warm place and was figuring out how to avoid going. She felt out of place and had no interest in the chitchat and politics of getting ahead. As for the future, her plans were to "work another five years and then teach third grade."

When I first met with Nancy shortly after the merger announcement, it was clear that, rebelliousness aside, she was successful. Although many others I interviewed at Fleet did fear for their jobs, Nancy did not. She knew that she had a position but was not sure what it would be. In fact, she had no voice in this decision: "I was locked out." Nancy's main concerns were not economic but more social, although that is not exactly the right word. She was close to her team and did not want to break it up. She also had a close relationship with her boss, who accepted her idiosyncrasies, and Nancy was afraid of not only losing that relationship but also finding herself competing with him. Like many of the people I interviewed, Nancy felt loyalty to her work and her work group and much less to the larger organization.

Although she did keep her job, the transition was not easy, and by our second conversation six months later, Nancy was distraught. The content of her job was "chopped up" and "blown apart" in the sense that rather than being responsible for a range of services to her clients, she had only one component. The job was narrower and in some sense de-skilled. Besides losing her old clients and her old team, she found herself in the "horrible" position of competing with her former boss for clients. She was ready to pack it in: "I think if you went around and asked people if they had a choice today whether they'd take a job or take a package, you'd get a fair number of people whose hands would be raised for the package—mine included."

In our final conversation six months later, the picture had changed yet again. She had been moved into another division of the bank and was in a new line of business. She had not regained the same degree of autonomy that she had before the merger ("I don't have as much independence as I did have. It's just different"), but she was much more accepting of the state of affairs. Thoughts of teaching third grade had gone by the boards ("I can't afford it"), and Nancy now had a cell phone, a Black-Berry, and an e-mail connection at home. In virtually all respects, she was happier and more committed, but some of the old Nancy remained. She had recently turned down a promotion chance because it involved travel and more hours and she did not want to lose the time at her weekend house, her tennis group, or too many of her evenings. On balance, however, Nancy was very much back on track and, in some respects, more hooked into the corporate life than before.

In several of our conversations, I asked Nancy about how she thought about restructuring, whether, for example, she believed

that layoffs were justified and how she felt about the high severance packages the members of top management were receiving
while others were losing their jobs. She had no broad political
critique. Nancy believed that "management has an obligation to
use its resources as best it can" and that "if an organization is
going to grow and thrive, you have to prune back every once in a
while." But even though she was generally accepting of the system in the large, in the small she was critical. She did not feel
close to top management, and some of the big packages upset
her and seemed undeserved.

Stepping back, we can see clearly that Nancy has gone
through the classic travails of the modern middle manager. Her
organization was bought and merged. Jobs were lost and others
were redesigned. New controls were imposed and a new culture
imported. Nancy was ready to walk out. Yet in the end, she has a
job that is in many respects good for her. Though not especially
loyal to the larger organization, she respects it. She also buys into
the values of efficiency that justify layoffs, yet she recognizes that
there is considerable abuse at the top. Is Nancy a victim or a
victor? The answer is not clear, and that lack of clarity is a more
accurate reflection of reality than the popular discussion.

HOW THIS BOOK IS ORGANIZED

As mentioned earlier, my goal in this book is to describe what
has happened to middle managers as firms restructure. To this
end, chapter 1 defined what middle managers are, explained
how the data on middle managers were obtained, and presented
some examples and explanations of common assumptions about

middle management. In chapter 2, I provide a context along two dimensions for understanding what has happened to managers. The chapter describes how the literature has viewed middle management and lays out the evolution of the managers' employment circumstances from the so-called golden age of middle managers to the current period, in which they are held in such (unjustified) contempt. Then in chapter 3, I use the national surveys to provide the basic facts regarding middle managers' employment, facts that are inconsistent with the popular image of middle management as a declining breed.

With this background in hand, I then ask about the corresponding transformation in the nature of work, the trajectory of careers, and the determinants of success and failure. Middle managers are "workers"; there is every reason to think that the nature of their work, the kinds of control that they experience, and what underlies their success has shifted in recent years. In chapter 4, I describe the evolution of managerial work and take up the shifting determinants of success. Chapter 5 examines the changing rules for success, who gets ahead, and who does not in the new regime.

The theme of chapter 6 is the commitment and loyalties of managers, to their work and to their organizations. My interviews strongly suggest that the managers are akin to craft workers, both enjoying what they do and committed to a high quality of work. A not-so-optimistic picture emerges, however, when I examine their relationship to their employers. The ties of mutual commitment between firms and managers seem to have frayed substantially. Has the Organization Man become the Organization Critic? How do managers think about their circumstances and the nature and responsibilities of firms? Are middle managers still loyal, and if so, to whom or what?

Finally, chapter 7 reflects on the shifting nature of managerial work and the consequences for people in these jobs. It asks about the meaning of managerial work in the new economic circumstances and whether we need to rethink our understanding of who managers are and what they do. It also examines policies that a firm might undertake to improve both the organizational outcomes and the work lives of its managerial employees. The fate and occupational trajectory of middle management has much in common with what is happening to other jobs throughout the society. All are being reshaped by new ideas regarding organizational design and by the sharper-edged competition that their employers confront. All are being forced to ask questions about where their loyalty lies and the meaning of their work. The story of middle managers is important in its own terms; these people, after all, make the economy run. But their story has a wider resonance in the new economy in which we must all make our way.

New Realities

The Shifting Context of
Middle Management

The emergence of management in general and middle management in particular is chronicled in the work of economic historian Alfred Chandler. Chandler writes about the importance of management in enabling economic growth and achieving the efficiencies of scale. The title of his book says it all: *The Visible Hand*. Instead of explaining the productivity of modern economies by referring to the power of the impersonal market and the benefits of the pricing system, as is the wont of conventional economics, Chandler argues that the deliberate actions of management are the heroes of the story.

Chandler tells the story in two stages. Early in the twentieth century, advances in technology permitted cheap production on a very large scale. To take advantage of this possibility, firms needed a marketing, sales, and distribution system that could effectively expand the market and handle large volumes. Building such a system required management, but in addition, an expanded management function was then needed to coordinate the production and distribution sides of the enterprise. Middle management, in Chandler's account, was the key actor that facilitated the remarkable growth and efficiency of the American economy. Without middle management's coordination of production and distribution, firms could not grow big enough to take advantage of the technological potential of mass production and low unit cost.

The second stage was the rise of the multidivisional firm. These organizations went beyond the traditional single-product-line business and instead incorporated multiple product lines under one group of senior managers. The role of top management in such a setup was planning and resource allocation, both of which required a substantial central management function. Once again, management emerges as the source of growth and efficiency.

A good illustration of the first stage is American Tobacco. Initially, the firm bought leaf from brokers that stored and cured the tobacco. Then, after it produced the cigarettes, the firm relied on independent wholesalers and advertising agents to sell the product. With the advent of the Bonsack machine, American Tobacco could produce at very high volumes and lower unit cost. To justify the expensive capital investment, the company required an integrated firm. As a result, the company established its own marketing and sales organization and then needed to coordinate production with demand in the field and to allocate production to different factories. It also had to control purchasing and packaging if large-scale production was to proceed smoothly. The goal was to enable the firm to engage in continuous mass production and hence drive costs down. Achieving all this required managers in the field to manage sales and distribution and central managers to coordinate flows.

Another illustration is the role of management in saving General Motors. Under its founder, William Durant, the firm experienced near bankruptcy in the downturn of 1920, when it lost control of its inventories (i.e., when production and distribution became unaligned). Much like the case of American Tobacco, more management was the solution to this coordination problem, and Alfred P. Sloan stepped in to help create the modern corporation.[1]

Sloan innovated by creating the multidivisional firm as the best way to manage an enterprise with multiple product lines. The simple idea was that top management operating at the center would allocate resources to the divisions most in need of them and monitor each division's progress. Meanwhile, each division would run its own show and handle the balancing problem of production and distribution described above. In fact, senior managers soon learned that substantial gains were to be had from cross-division planning, and as a result, a corps of middle management also emerged at the center. In General Motors, for example, the central staff and the division managers worked together in interdivisional relations committees on common problems and on planning.

In Chandler's telling, supported by detailed descriptions of specific firms, these managers, both in the center and in the divisions, improved economic efficiency. He lays out a central role for middle managers: "'Project program managers,' 'market program managers,' 'interface managers,' and 'scheduling managers' all helped to facilitate flows of material, funds, and ideas through the enterprise."[2] These managers were heroes, not bureaucratic obstacles or deadweight. They enabled large firms to grow while driving down unit costs through efficiencies of scale and better allocation of internal resources.

The growing importance of management to organizational success was reflected, as Chandler points out, in the professionalization of management as a career. Managers formed professional associations (e.g., the Administrative Management Association, established in 1919), professional journals were established, and business schools began their steady growth. Data on what might be termed the managerial intensity of firms support Chandler's story. For example, in 1923, at the meatpacking firm Swift and Company, there were 50,000 employees and 500 managers, whereas by 1950, there were 75,000 employees and 2,150 managers.[3] More generally, from 1900 to 1929, the ratio of administrative staff to production workers grew from 8.1 percent to 17.9 percent.[4]

In short, from the Chandlerian perspective, managers are heroes in that their functions facilitated growth and efficiency: "The tasks of middle management were entirely new. Middle managers had to pioneer in the ways of modern administrative coordination."[5]

CAREER PATTERNS IN THE GOLDEN AGE
OF MIDDLE MANAGEMENT

As managers became more important to organizations for the reasons explicated by Chandler, firms began to formalize their careers. Wharton School human resources expert Peter Cappelli describes the rise of what he terms "talent management" of managers and executives.[6] Even as the need for managers grew, firms in the early twentieth century preferred to poach talent from each other rather than develop their own. The original owner-managers of large enterprises had little appreciation of professional management and were content to simply hire outsiders if help was needed. This began to change with General Electric, under its new president, Gerard Swope, who led the charge in the 1920s. Swope established a one-year managerial training program that included both classroom training and systematic rotation among job assignments. This effort was expanded after the Depression and World War II, and a major training facility was built in Crotonville, New York. General Electric's planning for managerial development and career ladders was so deep that the firm developed succession planning and a "depth chart" of managers for thirty years into the future.

Other firms followed the GE example. For example, Sears, Roebuck and Co. tested over ten thousand young managers and established two fast tracks: a "Reserve Group" of five thousand managers and a "Special Reserve Group" of five hundred rapid risers. Standard Oil Company of California created for all its managers a "Personal Experience Record," which included a section that projected each manager's future career. The Conference Board, a well-known business group, estimated that in the 1950s, 60 percent of large firms had established formal management development programs.

What do we know about the actual outcomes for middle managers during their period of ascendancy? What were the patterns of mobility and advancement? Two widely spaced quantitative studies provide excellent bookend snapshots. The first is a report from the old AT&T managerial assessment program that followed a cohort of young managers who were hired between 1956 and 1960. The second is a more recent analysis of personnel data in a large financial services firm for the years 1969 to 1988. Together, the studies paint a very consistent picture, albeit one that is not entirely in tune with the extreme version of lifetime employment and the Organization Man.

The old AT&T system had one of the most elaborate management development systems in American businesses, not surprising, given the enormous size of the firm (200,000 managers at the peak), the science-based nature of the industry, and the ability to pass costs on to customers. One component of the system was an Assessment Center, which tested college recruits and attempted to predict the likely course of their careers. The psychologist Douglas Bray and his associates were asked by AT&T to study a sample of the college graduates who were hired as managerial trainees and who were put through the Assessment Center. The result was a valuable portrait of the progression of early managerial careers in an iconic American firm.[7] During this period, AT&T hired about 2,000 college graduates into its managerial ranks and promoted about 10,000 noncollege employees into first-level managerial jobs. Bray's Management Progress Study followed a sample of 274 white men hired from college between 1956 and 1960. The race and gender composition of the group reflected AT&T policy of that period, a policy that was challenged and blown apart by a consent decree signed in 1976 with the Equal Employment Opportunity Commission.

After the managers were hired and assessed, they were assigned to one of the Bell operating companies, and very few of the managers moved from that company. In this sense, the functional areas were rigid. However, the managers were also assigned to a particular department (Plant, Traffic, Commercial, or Engineering), and by the end of the eight years, just over half had changed departments at least once. So the system was somewhat less rigid than it might have appeared.

One striking finding was that, of the initial sample, 37 percent left the firm by the end of the eighth-year follow-up. It turns out that lifetime employment was not quite the norm. Of the people who had left, about half were voluntary and half had been gently or forcefully encouraged to depart. About a third of those who stayed made it to the third level.

A central question addressed by Bray and of great interest to those operating the Assessment Center was whether it was possible to predict who would do well and who would not. In this case, doing well meant, first, staying with the firm and not being counseled out and, second, achieving a third-level management position by the end of the eight years.

There is a strong bias in the economics and psychology literatures to attribute success to personal characteristics—ability, motivation, and the like. Conversely, sociologists are more open to the argument that opportunity and structure are important and that the same employee will do better or worse, depending on the circumstances in which the person finds himself or herself. Although he did not pose the question in these terms, Bray found support for both viewpoints. On the one hand, personnel at the Assessment Center were able, after only several days, to predict with a reasonable degree of accuracy who would be asked to leave the firm and who would make it to level three. On the other hand, an illustration of the role of opportunity and structure was that among those with positive predictions of promotion, the quality of the initial boss (in terms of training, providing opportunity for taking initiative, and the like) made a good deal of difference in the eventual outcome. There were also wide differences by operating company in the fraction of new hires who got promoted.

The fundamental fact, however, was that, of the large numbers of college recruits hired into managerial jobs, about two-thirds stayed with the firm for a long stretch. The careers of these long-termers were watched over and shaped by an elaborate system that involved careful assessment, observation, and systematic job rotation. Winners and losers were selected by the system, and there was every expectation that the winners would continue to compete for promotion whereas the progress of the losers would be slow.

These patterns were, perhaps surprisingly, also apparent in a more recent study of managerial careers.[8] In this case, the researchers had access to the personnel records over time for all managers of a medium-size national financial services firm between 1969 and 1988. Over these years, employment tripled and the authors observed the career patterns of people already at the firm and of new hires.

The first key observation was that like AT&T but unlike the most stylized version of the Organization Man, there was considerable turnover. The firm had eight managerial levels (level 8 being the CEO), and at each level except the very top, about 10 percent of the managers left every year. In addition, the job ladders were not closed to the outside: the growth in the firm was accomplished by substantial hiring at every level and not simply at the bottom.

Although the job ladders were more open, to both entry and exit, than the stylized image might suggest, the classic viewpoint was valid in other ways. While there was considerable turnover, 40 percent of the managers who were at level 1 at the beginning of the period ended up staying with the firm for ten years or more. The career paths themselves were very simple; the authors were able to collapse thousands of job titles into seventeen titles and eight levels, which accounted for virtually all employment. Furthermore, over this period, the structure was remarkably stable, hardly changing at all.

Particularly striking was how the upward-mobility process worked. The firm seemed to operate what was in effect a tournament in which people competed for promotions to the next level. The longer a manager waited for his or her next promotion, the less likely that, after the promotion, the person would receive yet another promotion. In other words, the promotion process seemed designed to pick out winners and losers. The winners, people on a fast track or even just a relatively speedy one, moved up from one level to the next and spent relatively little time at each level. The losers spent much more time at a level and were unlikely to move up yet again. In all respects, this service company has a career system very much like the one described at AT&T. It may be reasonable to conclude that together, these two studies provide a fair picture of managerial careers before the deluge.

In short, during the heyday of the Organization Man, managers enjoyed, as the popular image suggests, stable, long-term employment, although there was more turnover than the stereotype would imply. The career patterns themselves were relatively simple and straightforward, with movement up well-defined ladders housed in functional chimneys being the norm. Upward mobility was a reasonable expectation for many managers.

THE SEA CHANGE

From the mid-1980s onward, the Chandlerian managerial hero gave way to a quite different perception about the role of middle managers. Chandler's views notwithstanding, the tenor of the current discussion has shifted. What, then, is the other case—that they are villains? A dramatic way of posing this question is to contrast Chandler's story of how middle management saved General Motors from its failure to balance production and distribution with an employee's description of the nature of management at GM in more modern times: "Unless you're working on the fourteenth floor, you have about a zillion bosses. Every small thing requires approval up the line. They have thirteen thousand checkers in this company to make sure things are done right. Hell, they have checkers to check the checkers. It's madness."[9]

In this view, middle management expanded to the point that it is dysfunctional. Not only is it using up too many resources (i.e., collecting salaries for doing unproductive work), but it is actually an obstacle to efficient production. This perspective, ironically, is shared both by corporate raiders (recall Carl Icahn's chapter 1 quote about firing managers who report to managers) and by critics on the left. For example, the late economist David Gordon saw the growth of managers as a major explanation for the widening income inequality in America because their compensation sucked up profits that might otherwise go to raising the wages of frontline workers. To make his point, Gordon calculated what he termed the "bureaucratic burden" of U.S. firms, that is, the percentage of employees who were supervisors. His data show this "burden" increased steadily from about 12 percent just after World War II to 19 percent in the early 1990s. Although it levels off or drops slightly at the beginning of the 1990s, the major story is the steady upward climb.[10]

The most influential critique of middle managers is found in the iconic business book of the 1990s, Michael Hammer and James Champy's *Reengineering the Corporation*. In Hammer and Champy's view, great efficiencies in production and, more importantly, improved service to customers result when business activities are conceived of as processes and not as the sum of the coordinated actions of separate functional units (hence the term *process reengineering*). A canonical example of this is purchasing and inventory, and the authors give an example from Ford Motor Company.[11] In the bad old days, the purchasing department would send a purchase order to a vendor, and a copy went to the accounts payable department. When the goods arrived, someone at the receiving dock would fill out a form and send it to accounts payable. The vendor would also send an invoice. Accounts payable then had three pieces of paper and would make sure that they were consistent before sending a check. All of this was slow, required a lot of people, and was prone to error at a number of stages. It was also based on a functional division of labor, namely, a separate accounts payable department. Under the new system, when a purchase order is made, it is entered into a database. When the goods arrive at the dock, the receiving personnel check to see that the shipment is correct, and if it is, they simply enter a code into their computer and the payment check is automatically issued. The need for a separate accounts payable department is virtually eliminated. The mind-set that "we pay when we receive an invoice, and this needs to be dealt with by an accounts payable department" was the blockage, and it was overcome. Instead, the entire series of steps is thought of as a unified process, and the firm found the most efficient way to implement that process.

Hammer and Champy's book is full of examples of this sort, ranging from customer service to product development to manufacturing. The central theme is that middle managers, with their attachment to functional departments, are an obstacle and that there are simply too many managers in most firms. The authors are fundamentally hostile to middle managers and assert that when firms undergo reengineering, many managers should be eliminated: "Companies no longer require as much managerial 'glue' as they used to." The book portrays middle managers as narrow and deeply attached to their own functional turf: "Frontline managers embrace incrementalism because they can act incrementally without exceeding the range of their vision."[12]

The modern management literature is not uniform in its condemnation of middle management; one underground perspective praises middle managers or at least sees their value. This line of thought argues that middle managers can facilitate radical organizational change by helping to sell it to lower-level workers and by using their own deep knowledge of the organization to generate new ideas.[13] Nonetheless, the reengineering movement has been very popular and is widely used to justify the elimination of middle management positions. In corporate America today, the hostility of *Reengineering the Corporation* is far more prevalent than the hero worship of Chandler.

THE IBM STORY

Just how much has changed can be seen in the experience of one of America's best known firms, IBM. Long seen as the iconic representative of a managerial firm with a paternalistic system of lifetime employment, IBM initiated its first layoffs in the early 1990s. Between 1986 and 1994, worldwide employment at "Big Blue" fell from 407,000 to 215,000.[14] More fundamentally, all the rules of the managerial game changed as the firm systematically chose winners and losers from within its managerial ranks and permitted a growing dispersion of pay and other benefits.

The old IBM was consistently cited as one of the best employers in America, and its human resource policies were widely seen as exemplary. Its practices were driven by the philosophy articulated by Thomas Watson Jr., the son of the founder and an IBM CEO: "IBM seeks to provide a maximum degree of satisfaction on the part of its employees in their assigned tasks."[15] For many years, this philosophy seemed to pave the way to success as IBM dominated its industry and was immensely profitable. But when the competitive environment changed, the structure of managerial careers and the IBM human resources philosophy were exposed as an obstacle to success in the new world. IBM's administrative overhead costs were out of line with its competitors, but there were even more fundamental problems. The firm was unable to fire poor performers and instead simply transferred them to other units. Because the compensation system emphasized standard pay increases and narrow pay ranges, there was little scope for high-powered incentives. Bureaucratic empires had been built; seventeen levels of hierarchy lay between first-level supervisors and the CEO. Nimble decision making was impossible.

The new managerial world was ushered into IBM by Lou Gerstner, the perfect messenger of new realities. A Harvard Business School graduate and former McKinsey consultant, Gerstner had held senior positions at American Express and had headed up RJR Nabisco following the most famous leveraged buyout in history. In his account of his years at IBM, Gerstner in effect argues that the Chandlerian world had spun out of control. In Gerstner's view, the natural instincts of empire building interacted with perverse incentives and led to top-heavy bureaucratic organizations: "Today IBM has one Chief Information Officer. Back then we had, by actual count, 128 people with CIO in their titles—all of them managing their own local systems architectures and funding home-grown applications." He also describes the spirit of noncooperation in the company: "Research-and-development units would hide projects they were working on so other parts of the company would not learn of them and try to take advantage of their knowledge . . . [Under IBM's 'nonconcur system'] any individual, any team, any division [could] block agreement or action."[16]

In fact, senior managers may well have had an incentive to hire too many middle managers because the seniors' compensation depended on the size of their empire. A large body of literature demonstrates that when a top manager oversees more and more managers, then his or her compensation grows. By the same token, middle managers find it in their self-interest to expand their own mini-empires. The temptations facing managers stand as a reasonable explanation of the decline and fall of the Chandlerian managerial hero.

Managerial layoffs had begun prior to Gerstner's arrival, but he accelerated them. More importantly, he changed the rules of the game. Poor performers were fired. Compensation was transformed as he redesigned the performance assessment system and introduced pay for performance. He eliminated layers and axed the legions of staff with which senior executives had surrounded themselves. He also introduced a Darwinian system for identifying and working with managers: his Senior Leadership Group. These were the three hundred managers who appeared to be performing best and with whom he met several times a year. Every year, the membership of the group was reconsidered. Some people were asked, on the basis of their performance, to leave, and new members were added. Of the original three hundred, only seventy-two remained by the time Gerstner left the firm after his nine years of leadership.[17]

These changes transformed the lives and careers of thousands of managers, those who left and those who stayed. Job security was gone, the nature of the work had changed, and the basis of success had shifted. The old IBM, with its traditions and processes, was gone. The transformation, however wrenching, seemed necessary because of the fundamental shifts in the marketplace and because the IBM of old was ill equipped to respond. And the changes paid off. IBM stock, which stood at $11 in March 1993, soared to $125 in December 2001, shortly before Gerstner left.

After this dramatic reconfiguration of work and careers and after the success that followed, a reasonable expectation was that life would settle down into some kind of new and stable system. Remarkably, that has not happened. Indeed, the deeper lesson of the IBM story seems to be that change in the managerial world is perpetual.

The first sign of the permanently unsettled nature of the new managerial environment was IBM's efforts to redesign, and reduce, its pension commitments. The company began by substituting a cash-balance pension system for its old defined-benefits plan. Under defined benefits, which used to dominate America's pension schemes, the payout is back-loaded so that the longer one works at a firm, the better the pension. The cash-balance plan eliminates this feature and substitutes a constant payout over time, so that the benefits associated with, say, staying from year five to year six of job tenure are the same as from year twenty-nine to year thirty. Clearly, this plan reduced the gains associated with long-term employment. IBM endured a class-action lawsuit on behalf of its more senior employees, but the plan was upheld. But this was not enough for the company. In 2006, IBM eliminated the cash-balance plan altogether and put in its place a 401(k) plan in which the firm's only commitment was its annual contribution (a generous one by national standards). In effect, the pension risk was shifted to the workforce.

One goal of these shifts was clearly to save money; the estimates pointed to several billion dollars in savings over just a few years. However, there was a deeper motive. The transformation of the pension system both signaled and reinforced the fundamental shift in the nature of employment. In a memo to employees explaining the rationale of the pension shift, the head of IBM's human resources department was clear: "For much of IBM's history, 30-year careers were the norm. That career model is still viable for some, but it's no longer predominant."[18]

IBM's pension move was far from unique. For example, at about the same time, Verizon also revised the pension system for its managers by ending its defined-benefits plan and shifting to a 401(k). The CEO explained the change in language that could have been taken from the IBM playbook: "This restructuring reflects the realities of our changing world."[19]

The IBM human resources philosophy echoes the new mantra that employees are responsible for their own careers and that, at most, the firm's role is to provide a chance to learn. "It's very much a trust-responsibility equation," is how the vice president for human resources described the firm's strategy of identifying hot skills and offering employees a chance to get the appropriate training.[20]

Indeed, the firm recently announced that it will innovate by establishing "individual learning accounts" for its employees.[21] As it does for retirement accounts, the firm will match a fraction of the employees' contribution. The funds will be portable and may be used for retraining not simply for another job at IBM but for jobs elsewhere. CEO Samuel J. Palmisano is explicit that the benefit will make the firm "more competitive" because it will be able to attract employees despite its inability to promise long-term jobs. A portion of the burden of this benefit will be borne by the firm—fifty cents on every dollar that an employee contributes up to one thousand dollars—but a much larger portion will, of course, be borne by the worker. As the CEO remarked, "It puts the right balance of motivation into the system. Everyone has some skin in the game." Regardless of who is bearing the cost and benefits, the door has long since closed on the old IBM employment system, and the company is charging into the new world.

The new pension and training philosophies are one signal that the new IBM created by Gerstner meant continual change and was not a simple onetime shift. The more profound evidence of this is top leadership's new conception of the firm and the opening of its labor force to the world. In a series of speeches, Palmisano made it clear that the nature of the firm had changed: "We're moving beyond 'international' business to something that is more like 'transnational.'" He explained that in this "globally integrated enterprise . . . work flows to where it is done best . . . based on the right cost, the right skills, and the right business environment."[22] At the time of these remarks, IBM had fifty-three thousand employees in India and had just announced a three-year investment of $6 billion in that nation, double the previous three years' $3 billion investment. IBM had moved far beyond treating India and other nations as sources of cheap labor for back-office operations.

The point of this for IBM's managers is clear. They are competing for their jobs with skilled talent from all over the world, and in the explicit words of IBM's CEO, the fact that they are American conveys no advantage in the calculations of the firm. As another illustration of this point, as of May 2007, IBM had laid off over thirty-seven hundred employees for the calendar year. The old world of IBM, which lasted for half a century, has been blasted away, but the new world is not stable. Instead, IBM managers face seemingly permanent uncertainty and risk.

IMAGES IN THE LITERATURE

Managers are at the core of how social science views modern society and the modern economy. In his brilliant 1956 essay, "Work and Its Discontents," Daniel Bell identified the central features of the modern firm as size and hierarchy. Taken together, these add up to management. In making this point, Bell was drawing on the work of Max Weber, the founder of modern sociology. Weber viewed bureaucracy as the logical final step of an organizational trajectory that went from personalistic or charismatic leadership to simple authoritarianism to the impersonal rules and carefully defined duties of a bureaucrat.

Despite Weber's and Bell's implicit respect of middle management, many other images of middle managers in the social science literature have been broadly negative. This trend arises from a longstanding tradition of social science writing that sees middle managers as victims and pawns. Joseph Heller and, before him, Franz Kafka are representative of the literary world. The flavor of their views pervades much social science and popular writing on the evils of bureaucracy and the dispiriting impact of large organizations on their denizens.

The view that middle managers are victims has a long social science provenance. As his major project in the 1950s, the famous Columbia University sociologist C. Wright Mills mapped the emerging American class structure. He identified what he termed the "power elite" who ran the nation, and he wrote powerfully enough about them to turn the label into a popular catchphrase. He also turned his critical gaze to the nation's growing army of white-collar workers and sought to identify them as a new class. His conception of the class was broad, ranging from clerks and salespeople to middle managers. Then he turned to middle managers:

> As with any "middle" group, what happens to the middle managers is largely dependent on what happens to those above and below them—to top management and to foremen. The pace and character of work in the middle management are coming increasingly to resemble those in the lower ranks of the management hierarchy . . . middle managers become the routinized general staff without final responsibility and decision . . . He is always somebody's man . . . and he is seen as the man who does not rise and is pushed by forces beyond his control.[23]

This view of middle managers continued to dominate the popular imagination. The journalist William H. Whyte captured this perspective in *Organization Man*: "They are not the workers, nor are they the white-collar people in the usual, clerk sense of the word. These people not only work for The Organization. The ones I am talking about *belong* to it as well. They . . . have left home, spiritually as well as physically, to take the vows of organizational life."[24]

The expression *organization man* entered the national vocabulary, but in fact Whyte's argument was deeper than simply a concern about conformity in managerial ranks. His story was about the increased collectivization in American society and the glorification of the group. The book contains extended attacks on many of the techniques, such as personality testing and communications strategies, that characterize modern "human resource management."

Modern proponents of the manager-as-victim view take two somewhat distinct positions. One is the straightforward focus on layoffs and insecurity and the seemingly new class of managerial victims as firms restructure. In the mid-1990s, the *New York Times* ran a multipart blockbuster series, "Downsizing of America," the first article of which began with this doom-laden pronouncement: "Job apprehension has intruded everywhere, diluting self-worth, splintering families, fragmenting communities, altering the chemistry of workplaces, roiling political agendas and rubbing salt on the very soul of the country."[25] A later article in the series chronicled the situation of James E. Sharlow, a $130,000-per-year manager at Eastman Kodak Company who lost his job as the firm downsized and who commented, "I believe in the American Dream. I feel it fading."[26]

The impact of the newly insecure world on the psyche of managers is explored in greater depth and with an even greater sense of tragedy by the sociologist Richard Sennett, who aptly, given the viewpoint, titles his book *The Corrosion of Character*, a corrosion brought about by what he terms (the new) "flexible capitalism." Sennett begins his book by recounting a conversation he had with a manager who happened to be the son of someone whom he had interviewed for an earlier book. The rootlessness and sense of loss that this manager articulated frames the entire argument. The problem is not simply that people suffer economically but rather that the very meaning of their life is lost. Sennett believes there is "no long term" in the modern economy and that the economy "rejects careers . . . as pathways along which people can travel; durable and sustained paths of action are foreign." The consequence is that people can no longer make good sense of their lives: "What is missing . . . is a narrative . . . [The] world is marked by short-term flexibility and flux; this world does not offer much, either economically or socially, in the way of narrative . . . the conditions of the time in the new capitalism have created a conflict between character and experience, the experience of disjointed time threatening the ability of people to form characters into sustained narratives."[27]

Sennett is a social commentator very much in the tradition of C. Wright Mills, yet ironically seems to mourn the loss of the old corporate world, the world of the Organization Man. In that older world, according to him, people's lives had meaning and a sense of sustained narrative. They could explain to their children what they did and why they did it, and they could promise their children a similar future. What Heller in fiction and Whyte in journalism and Mills in social science all viewed as stultifying, Sennett evidently (and perhaps inadvertently, given his earlier writing) views as a paradise lost. Although the weight of popular and scholarly opinion sees middle managers as victims, this view is not unanimous. Other observers believe that the new organizational architecture fundamentally changed the nature of middle management for the better. The new world is characterized in different terms, for example, the "post entrepreneurial workplace" or the "boundaryless career."[28] Whatever the terminology, all writers in this line agree that the weight of bureaucracy has been lifted and new opportunities are in the offing. Instead of being the automatons portrayed in the novels and popular books such as *The Organization Man*, middle managers of modern enterprises are invited to become "intrapreneurs," to take charge of their careers, and to express their creativity. One view (using the kind of phrase making that is typical in this literature) claims that "by the beginning of the 1990's it was clear that the Third-Wave revolution had driven many careers out of the middle of large pyramidal hierarchies and replaced them with new careers in which people work across the boundaries of small networked companies."[29]

Rosabeth Moss Kanter thinks that "climbing the career ladder is being replaced by hopping from job to job. Reliance on organizations to give shape to a career is being replaced by reliance on self."[30] She highlights "Paul," who would never go back to middle management now that he is an "internal venture capitalist." Other middle managers become professionals, with advancement coming from an increase in skill, not hierarchy, and yet others are intrapreneurs. What Sennett sees as tragedy these commentators see as opportunity.

In this view, the organizational redesign that seems at first glance to undermine job security is really an opening for middle managers to find new roles and to manage their own growth and careers in ways that had never before been permitted. Even James Champy, one of the architects of reengineering, bought into this view: "We are in the grip of the second managerial revolution . . . The first was about the transfer of power. This one is about an access of freedom."[31]

CONCLUSION

Both the circumstances and the perception of middle managers have evolved. During the era in which the modern economy was built, they were heroes. During the post–World War II period, they were victims. When restructuring took hold, they became villains. Reality, of course, is much more complex than these cardboard images.

Certainly, the negative perception of middle managers that pervades much of today's popular literature and social science writing is belied by the central role these managers have played in building strong and productive firms and, as we will see, by the nature of their current work and their attitudes toward their jobs. The same reality also undermines the more slogan-oriented advocates of "boundaryless careers" and "intrapreneurship." Nonetheless, as the example of IBM illustrates, much has changed.

The first step in understanding what has really happened is to see what the data say. In the next chapter, I examine nationally representative surveys to understand whether the ranks of middle managers have grown or declined in recent years and whether the managers' work has become more or less secure. I also ask about the changing gender composition of management and about trends in middle management compensation. With these facts in hand, we will then be able to bring a more reality-based understanding of the circumstances of middle management to bear on the core questions that drive this book.

Middle Management by the Numbers

What Do the Data Show?

As we just saw in chapter 2, the image of middle managers has evolved and has recently taken a real beating. Adding to their woes is that the drumbeat of news reports of downsizing combines with the reengineering rhetoric to create the impression that the managers are taking numerous blows and must be down for the count. But anecdotes, no matter how powerful, may not capture the realities in an economy as large and diverse as ours. What do the data show?

From the perspective of the entire economy, it is hard to see managers as victims. In 2007, adding wages and benefits, managers earned an average of fifty-seven dollars an hour, compared with twenty-seven an hour for all workers.[1] The unemployment rate of managers in 2007 was 1.7 percent, compared with the overall rate of 4.9 percent.[2] As a group, managers have the highest average job tenure of any occupation. Even when managers are laid off, they do better than other employees do. A survey reported in the *Wall Street Journal* found that in 2005, "non-senior" managers receive a median maximum severance package of twenty-eight weeks' salary, an increase of two weeks since 2001.[3] On these economic dimensions, managers are clearly a privileged group, hardly victims.

Despite these observations, in the context of their previous status and expectations, it is possible that the lot of managers has worsened. Virtually every merger or restructuring announcement brings with it promises by the architects to save money by cutting managerial ranks. The new vocabulary of *downsizing, delayering,* and *right-sizing* all speak to this urge. The data provide some support for these impressions. The U.S. Census Bureau conducts regular surveys on displaced workers, who are defined as employees with three or more years of tenure on their job and who lost that job due to plant or company closing, insufficient work, or abolition of their position or shift. In the latest survey of all those who were displaced between January 2001 and December 2003, 17 percent were classified in the occupation "management, business, or financial operations." Since employees in this grouping accounted for 10 percent of overall employment, managers seem to be taking a disproportionate share of the hit.[4]

This dislocation is reflected in the changing nature of layoffs. Increasingly, layoffs today are ways of restructuring and not simply responses to the business cycle. In earlier research, I assembled all the reports of layoffs noted in the *Wall Street Journal* for two years, 1972 and 1994, and classified them as layoffs due to poor current results or layoffs due to reorganization and structural change.[5] The year 1994 had a sharp increase in the relative proportion due to structural change. This research was replicated and improved on by Kevin Hallock, who examined all layoffs reported in the *Wall Street Journal* for *Fortune* 500 companies between 1970 and 2000.[6] He found a near tripling of layoffs due to restructuring, from 9.6 percent of the layoffs in the 1970s to 24.2 percent in the 1990s.

Given all the talk of removing managerial layers, one simple measure of what is happening to managers is their numbers. If firms are indeed cutting back on their managerial workforce, then we would expect to see a decline in the fraction of employment that is managers. On the other hand, if managers are, despite the tenor of the popular press, holding their own, then their employment fraction should be stable or even rising. Recall that during the Chandlerian era, the fraction of the workforce that was managers rose sharply, reflecting the rise of corporations and the increased importance of managers in making these new organizations function. For example, we saw that in the first two decades of the twentieth century, the nonproduction staff of firms doubled. What is happening now?

A Note on Data

Throughout this book, I will use nationally representative data from two sources. The first source is data collected in the monthly household surveys that the U.S. Bureau of the Census conducts. In different months and in different years, the census asked about occupations, job tenure, and wages of the respondents. These surveys have the great advantage of having a very large sample size and being nationally representative. They do, however, have several disadvantages. One is that the occupational classifications are less than perfect. Because the classification system used by the census has changed over this period, it is hard to compare apples to apples with confidence if the various definitions are stitched together to construct a long series. In addition, each of the classification schemes makes some odd decisions, or at least not useful ones, about what to include in the managerial category. For example, funeral directors are classified as managers under most of the schemes. Perhaps more seriously, under any of the household survey classification systems, the answers depend on self-reporting. Some people may exaggerate their importance and call themselves managers. Others who actually perform managerial jobs may instead report that they are, for example, engineers even though their real job is to manage groups of engineers.

To deal with the changing classification schemes, I report data separately for two periods: first for 1983 to 2002 and then for 2000 to 2006. Within each of these periods, the definition was constant (in the years 2000–2002, both definitions were available). In addition, I limit these data to people who are paid on a salaried basis as opposed to those paid an hourly wage. For those who are interested, the following paragraphs include more detailed technical information on how I have prepared the data and defined managers.

The data on the percentage of the labor force that is management, the wage rates of managers, and the percentage of women managers are all taken from the Current Population Survey, a monthly survey of households conducted by the Bureau of Census for the Bureau of Labor Statistics. To avoid using the same person twice, I use data only from month four (also known in Bureau of Labor Statistics lingo as the Outgoing Rotation Group). The sample is limited to employees who are ages twenty to sixty-four, salaried, not self-employed, and in the private sector. Managers are defined as occupation codes 7–22 for the pre-2000 data and 10–430 for the post-2000 data. That is, only managers are counted, not "management related" occupations. The suggested sample weights are used. For the wage data, I trimmed extreme values, as suggested by Thomas Lemieux, and I do not use allocated wages.[a] The data on job tenure comes from the relevant January and February Current Population Survey supplements. In these data, hourly versus salaried information is not available, so managers (using the same occupation codes described above) are limited to people with college education.

The second set of surveys that I use is the Quality of Employment Survey (QES, conducted by the University of Michigan in 1977 and sponsored by the U.S. Department of Labor) and the National Study of the Changing Workforce (conducted by the Families and Work Institute in 1997 and 2002 and sponsored by several foundations).[b] Although the National Study was executed in both English and Spanish, the QES was only in English. For the sake of comparison, I used only the English interviews. The data are limited to private-sector employees between the ages of twenty-five and sixty-four.

The National Study of the Changing Workforce replicated the QES and added questions. All these surveys contain much more detailed information than does the U.S. Census on the nature of people's work and have the additional advantage of enabling me to compare responses over a long period. The weakness of these data is that the sample sizes are obviously smaller than the census and hence produce greater statistical noise. To increase the sample size, I combine the 1997 and 2002 surveys.

a. Thomas Lemieux, "Increasing Residual Wage Inequality: Compositional Effects, Noisy Data, or Rising Demand for Skill," *American Economic Review* 96, no. 3 (June 2006): 461–498.

b. For the QES, see R. P. Quinn and G. L. Staines, *The 1977 Quality of Employment Survey* (Ann Arbor: Institute for Social Research, University of Michigan, 1979). For the 1997 and 2002 surveys, see J. T. Bond, E. Galinsky, and J. E. Swanberg, *The 1997 National Study of the Changing Workforce* (New York: Families and Work Institute, 1998), and J. T. Bond et al., *Highlights of the 2002 National Study of the Changing Workforce* (New York: Families and Work Institute, 2003).

Figure 3-1 shows the percentage of private-sector workers between ages twenty and sixty-four who report themselves as managers in the U.S. Census surveys over the years 1983–2002; figure 3-2 is for the period 2000–2006.

What is striking, even stunning, about these data is that the percentage of the labor force that is managerial shows a steady increase. This is in sharp contrast to what we would expect from the rhetoric about slashing managerial layers in firms. Of course, many firms may indeed be laying off managers, but evidently, other firms are hiring them to take up the slack.

One possible explanation for the increase in managerial intensity is that it is really a reflection of the changing industrial mix of the economy and not of what is happening within particular firms. Perhaps these data simply reflect a shift in the economy toward more "managerial" sectors even though, within each sector, fewer managers are being used. To test this, consider figures 3-3 and 3-4, which show the percentage of managers over time within manufacturing and within finance, insurance, and real estate. If the compositional story were true, we would expect to see a decline within each sector.

It turns out, however, that the same pattern is replicated within industries. Within manufacturing, the fraction of employment that is managerial has grown substantially. This doubtlessly reflects the relentless layoffs of blue-collar workers, which have led to a reconfiguration of employment proportions. However,

FIGURE 3-1

Percentage of private-sector workers between ages twenty and sixty-four who report themselves as salaried managers, 1983–2002

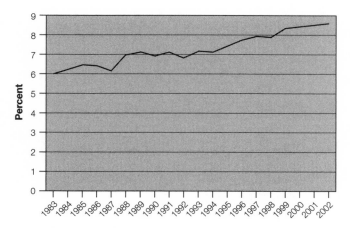

Source: Data from U.S. Census Bureau for the Bureau of Labor Statistics, *Current Population Survey,* a monthly survey of households, http://stats.bls.gov/cps/. See "A Note on Data" in this chapter for further details.

there is no comparable layoff story for the finance sector, where we also observe a milder, but nonetheless perceptible, growth of managerial employment.

As I noted, the census definition of managers leaves something to be desired, but we can probe more deeply by asking what percentage of people perform managerial functions even though these workers may not call themselves managers. A core function of managers is, obviously, supervision.[7] The Quality of Employment Survey (1977) and the National Study of the Changing Workforce (both the 1997 and the 2002 replications) asked respondents whether supervising people was a major part of their job. If we limit ourselves to white-collar employees who

FIGURE 3-2

Percentage of private-sector workers between ages twenty and sixty-four who report themselves as salaried managers, 2000–2006

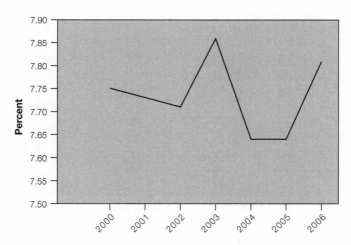

Source: Data from U.S. Census Bureau for the Bureau of Labor Statistics, *Current Population Survey*, a monthly survey of households, http://stats.bls.gov/cps/. See "A Note on Data" in this chapter for further details.

FIGURE 3-3

Percentage of managers within two industries, 1983–2002

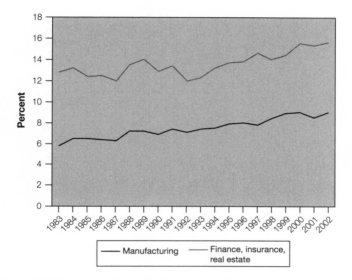

Source: Data from U.S. Census Bureau for the Bureau of Labor Statistics, *Current Population Survey*, a monthly survey of households, http://stats.bls.gov/cps/. See "A Note on Data" in this chapter for further details.

responded affirmatively and who were paid on a salaried basis, then 20.3 percent of the workforce was managerial in 1977 and 18.9 percent in 2002. These numbers are statistically equivalent. While we do not see the kind of striking increase that was apparent in the census data, there is no decline, as popular discussion would lead us to expect, and the percentage of employees who are managerial is notably higher than census figures.

WHAT HAS HAPPENED TO JOB TENURE?

If the career paths of managers have been transformed or, at a minimum, shaken up, then we could reasonably expect to see this reflected in the pattern of job tenure, that is, data on the length of

FIGURE 3-4

Percentage of managers within two industries, 2000–2006

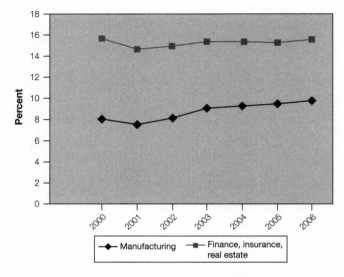

Source: Data from U.S. Census Bureau for the Bureau of Labor Statistics, *Current Population Survey*, a monthly survey of households, http://stats.bls.gov/cps/. See "A Note on Data" in this chapter for further details.

time that people spend with a particular employer. What can we say about how long today's managers stay with their employers and how this has changed in recent years? Every several years, the U.S. Census asks respondents, "How many years have you continuously worked with your current employer?" From their responses, we can calculate job tenure.[8] In the tables that follow, I combine the data from both men and women because I am interested in the overall trend for managerial jobs. In chapter 5, I will look at the divergent trends for the two genders.

A useful first question is to simply ask about the distribution of job tenure among managers today. Table 3-1 shows the pattern

In addition, from the early 1980s until the beginning of the new century, managerial compensation not only held its own but actually improved relative to the rest of the labor force. The gain of managers relative to the rest of the labor force reflected an actual increase in managerial compensation and not simply stagnation or decline elsewhere. Evidently, whatever the turmoil in other aspects of managerial life, when it came to earnings, managers continued to enjoy their somewhat protected position. Since the year 2000, however, the median pay of managers has stagnated. Although the beginning of the new century witnessed the dot-com crash and September 11, overall this was a period in which productivity grew sharply and corporate profits were more than healthy. Nevertheless, the average worker did not share in these gains, and neither did the average manager. In this sense, managers have lost their privileged status, although, of course, their wages remain well above average.

FIGURE 3-6

Ratio of median managerial wages to wages of all other employees, 2000–2006

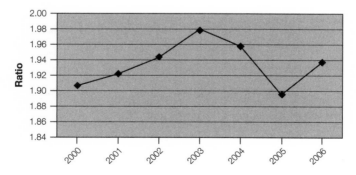

Source: Data from U.S. Census Bureau for the Bureau of Labor Statistics, *Current Population Survey*, a monthly survey of households, http://stats.bls.gov/cps/. See "A Note on Data" in this chapter for further details.

GENDER

Historically, management, like other professions, has been largely closed to women. But just as law and medicine are opening up, so is management. What percentage of managers are women? This seemingly simple question has no simple answer, in part because the data themselves are fuzzy and in part because a key second question is, What level of manager is being discussed? We can begin to get at this question using the same census data that I used earlier to track the percentage of overall employment that is managerial. Figures 3-7 and 3-8 show how the percentage of women managers varied between 1983 and 2006. (Recall from "A Note on Data" that managers are defined slightly differently in the Census surveys that underlie the two charts; hence, for the early 2000s, the years in which the charts

FIGURE 3-7

Percentage of managers who are women, 1983–2002

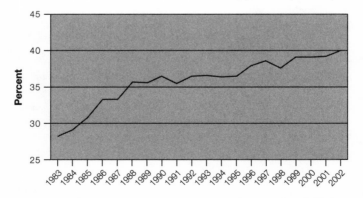

Source: Data from U.S. Census Bureau for the Bureau of Labor Statistics, *Current Population Survey*, a monthly survey of households, http://stats.bls.gov/cps/. See "A Note on Data" in this chapter for further details.

overlap, the figures are slightly different in each chart. This does not change the underlying story.)

There has been a steady increase in the percentage of women managers, from just over a quarter at the beginning of the 1980s to nearly 40 percent by 2006. This pattern is consistent with women's parallel success in obtaining access to other high-prestige occupations, such as lawyers and doctors. It is also worth noting that this pattern holds if we use our more functional definition of managers. When I define a manager in the National Study of the Changing Workforce as someone who is paid on a salaried basis and reports that supervising people is a major part of the job, then, in the 2002 survey, 43 percent of the managers were women.[10]

The progress that women have made moving into the managerial ranks is impressive. There remains, of course, a question

FIGURE 3-8

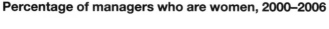

Percentage of managers who are women, 2000–2006

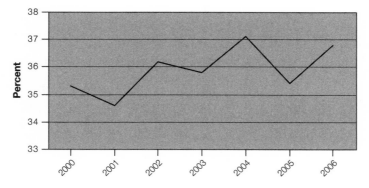

Source: Data from U.S. Census Bureau for the Bureau of Labor Statistics, *Current Population Survey,* a monthly survey of households, http://stats.bls.gov/cps/. See "A Note on Data" in this chapter for further details.

about their wages and promotion prospects. These questions will be addressed in chapter 5.

CONCLUSION

Stepping back and looking at these data yields a paradoxical picture. Job security is down, and as we will shortly see, stress is up. However, the number of managers in the economy is steadily increasing, not decreasing. This steady rise maintains the pattern followed during the entire twentieth century and shows no sign of reversing. The middle managers who are the heroes of Alfred Chandler's narrative may well have gone too far in feathering their nests, hence the dysfunction at IBM, but middle management is in no way disappearing from the scene.

The story told by the numbers cannot capture how life inside organizations has changed for middle managers. We have already seen that firms are under intense pressure and are responding by reshaping and reorganizing themselves. The restructuring has had objective consequences for managers in the kind of work they do, their job security, and their opportunities for advancement. We are left with questions about how reorganizations have changed the actual work that middle managers do. Have managers been "de-skilled" as organizations rationalize their operations, or have these people been empowered as layers of bureaucracy are peeled away? Are their jobs better or worse? Can they advance up their organization's hierarchies? These are the questions that I take up in the next chapters.

4

The Changing Role of Middle Management

What's New at Work?

"Robert," an information technology manager, was an English teacher in his late twenties when he entered a manager development program at one of the banks in the food chain leading to Fleet and then Bank of America. Now around fifty years old, Robert reported that he still had enough of the English teacher in him to prefer reading Sophocles than Gates. He did, however, go to school at night to get his MBA because he felt that the "business side" was becoming as important as the "technology side" in his job.

Our first conversation focused mainly on the nature of his job and how it had changed over time. Robert told the story of boundaries blurring, of fixed assignments giving way to teams, of technology driving change but also being intermingled with business considerations. "Ten to fifteen years ago, I knew what it was to be a manager. It was structured, job descriptions were clear, the skill sets were clear. Nowadays, the job description is as if the Delphic Oracle wrote it. What does that mean? It gets outdated quickly. Tech guys now spend more time in the business world. You can't be a geek now." What this means is that Robert now spends as much of his time working in ad hoc teams as he does on his main assignments, and the people who report to him do the same. Under the team system, reporting is matrixed and hence both Robert and his subordinates are responsible to multiple people. It also means his job requires him to negotiate business relationships with external parties, not simply manage or evaluate technology.

Despite all these changes, Robert was comfortable with his work. He enjoyed the technology and "working with a good team." Perhaps not as ambitious as before, he still saw opportunities for growth. But by our second conversation, Bank of America had begun to reconfigure his world, and by the third conversation, the pain had only intensified.

Robert was fortunate in that he kept his job. But he began our second conversation by observing, "I have been mapped." Several months later, he commented, "I submit the dreaded metrics once a month." The hot management techniques of Six Sigma and Total Quality Management (TQM) had begun to shape his work. The work itself had become narrower and more controlled. His new (and remote) manager wanted "one throat to choke." "Suddenly, my skill sets have been shaved, if you will, and focused on some very narrow problems . . . I have less autonomy; I have to double-check everything carefully."

The second and third conversations with Robert felt like a long howl of pain. Some loyalties remained: "I'm loyal to my manager, his group . . . these are my guys in the foxhole . . . OK, I understand where the corporation is going, but the real loyalties are at the working group level." But the conversations were full of references to Michael Moore, to the movie *Supersize Me*, and to a generally cynical view of the corporate world. All this was a far cry from the relatively upbeat first interview. At the same time, Robert saw no alternative but to go along. He drew no lessons, political or otherwise, from what had happened to his work and to his career.

The ending of the story (or at least the trajectory) was not happy for Robert, and his experience is indeed representative of many middle managers. But it is not the only outcome. Many other middle managers are able to navigate the changes in their environment and in their work and arrive at a happier resolution.

"Mary," a lender at Bank of America, had eighteen years of experience first at Bank of Boston and then at Fleet and was adept at protecting herself. As the merger with Bank of America played out, her boss introduced her to the Bank of America people and she followed up by sending them material describing her work and "calling, calling, calling." She ended up with more autonomy than she had before:

I have become much more autonomous for two reasons: one, there was some major management change above

me, early on. And [after I took] on this position, my
manager left, and then I was kind of out of a manager for
about six months, effectively. My new manager came in
and really had many other, more important projects that
he was working on, so that by default, I was able to just
do my thing and kept him apprised enough to make him
feel comfortable that I was in control.

The point to take away from Robert's and Mary's experience
is not the judgmental one of whether the world of middle managers is changing for the better or the worse. The answer is obviously complex, and we need to build up to an answer. But clearly,
restructuring is changing the nature of middle management
work. I begin in this chapter by asking what the core functions
or tasks of middle managers are. I then distinguish between the
ideas of breadth and autonomy and ask whether the work has
gotten broader or narrower over time and whether middle managers are subject to more top-down control than in the past.

MANAGERIAL WORK

There is a rich literature on what managers do, on what constitutes managerial work. The starting point is the writing of the
great German sociologist Max Weber. He developed the first
full-blown analysis of how bureaucracies operated and was, not
surprisingly, very much influenced by the German civil service
and armed forces. In his description of bureaucracy, managers
command and are obeyed. Their power flowed from their
position, and all denizens of the bureaucracy understood and
followed the commands, provided that the superiors respected

the rules of the institution. The implications for understanding managerial work were straightforward. What a manager did was to formulate strategy and supervise its execution. Put differently, managers made decisions and had them carried out. Rational planning and careful strategy formulation were the rules of the day. A more practical version of this view comes from a classic text published in 1938 by a senior AT&T executive and is still widely cited: "The essential executive functions . . . are, first, to provide the system of communication; second to promote the securing of essential efforts; and, third, to formulate and define purpose."[1] To decision making is added motivation and communication, but the manager is still seen as an army commander whose daily life would presumably consist of making decisions and issuing orders.

In fact, the thrust of virtually all organizational literature has been to push away from this view. The observation of one scholar of managerial work captures the spirit of the critique: "The iron law of American bureaucratic practice echoes in the refrain 'There's always a way around the rule—look for it.'"[2] The point is that the informal system dominates the formal one. Indeed, when it comes to thinking about what managers actually do, realism has gained the upper hand. Peter Drucker notes that "every manager does things that are not managing. He may spend most of his time on them."[3] And this is certainly true of middle managers who have loans to execute, circuits to design, and so on. But an even deeper critique challenges the idea of managers setting strategy from on high. Henry Mintzberg followed a set of managers around in their daily work and identified ten roles that constituted their professional lives: these were leader, disseminator of information, monitor, figurehead, liaison, spokesperson, entrepreneur, disturbance handler, resource allocator, and negotiator. In terms of how they acted out these roles, there was little in the way of quiet contemplation followed by strategy formulation. Instead, Mintzberg says, "the manager's activities are characterized by brevity, variety, and fragmentation . . . A great variety of activities are performed, but with no obvious patterns . . . There is great fragmentation of work."[4]

While most literature focuses on those at the top, the role of middle managers is often overlooked. It is clear that middle managers are responsible for accomplishing the core tasks of their organizations. These people get the circuits designed, place the loans, sell the product, oversee space allocation, manage legal issues, and handle all the many other core blocking and tackling tasks that together constitute the work of their organizations. In this respect, middle managers differ from senior managers, who are more concerned with strategy, resource allocation, and agenda setting. Nonetheless, when one steps back and looks at the day-to-day work of middle managers, one sees several core themes that can be abstracted from their concrete tasks. Middle managers are responsible for both internal and external management of teams, act as the transmission belt between the top of the organization and the bottom, and make day-to-day choices and trade-offs that escape the attention of top management yet are central to the organization's performance.

Teams

Teams today are central to how work is done, but teamwork means something different from the broad, vague idea of being a friendly colleague. Throughout organizations, project teams are increasingly seen as the best way to organize work. They bring together disparate skills to solve a problem, and many teams are disbanded and re-formed as the demands of the work changes. Other teams may be more permanent, but are task oriented.

Mintzberg famously compared cycles of management "innovations" to seasonal changes in the hemlines of dresses, but teams are the new mantra in organizations, for a good reason. Richard Hackman, one of the nation's leading researchers on teams, points out that teams have more resources, enjoy more flexibility, have more diverse ideas to draw from, and allow their members to learn from each other.[5] Teams have become so common that many of the current crop of best-selling business books focus on how to design and manage them. Any excursion into the library will find several shelves full of both research-oriented and how-to books on teams.

The term *team*, of course, includes many variants. Researchers study sports teams, performing arts groups, nurses in operating rooms, and pilots in cockpits. These are all in a real sense teams. Firms like TechCo organize project teams and cross-functional teams. Project teams are just what they sound like: groups brought together for the life of a project to work on a problem. Some project teams consist entirely of people in the same field, but others are cross-functional, that is, a team might involve engineers, marketing staff, production people, and so on. Virtually all the work in TechCo is now done via these teams. In Bank of America, teams are less universal but are nonetheless common. Some are the more traditional teams in which a leader (e.g., Nancy, the Fleet lending manager discussed in chapter 1) manages his or her group of lenders. But the ad hoc and cross-functional varieties are also common.

In manufacturing settings, teams have spread for two important reasons. First, they help engage employees more fully in their work by providing them more discretion in the workplace. Second, teams improve efficiency by making their members multiskilled so that backup workers are not needed during a team member's absence. These motives are less relevant in Bank of America and TechCo. However, teams in these settings meet a different set of needs. At TechCo, teams are responses to the environmental and technological uncertainty described earlier. By creating teams, the organization is able to pool the skills of multiple people, no single one of whom is likely to know enough to solve the increasingly complex problems the company faces. The teams are formed and re-formed because the nature of the challenges, and hence the particular collection of skills needed, is a moving target. When work is organized in this fashion, the teams can expand and contract over their lifetime as the project moves through different stages. At Bank of America, a branch manager commented that the increased size of teams was a function of the growing complexity of the work: "I think your teams are becoming more diverse in the case of the memberships. Because everybody is more of an expert and a specialist, so when you have teams together, it usually is a broader team."

One manager at TechCo explained the spread of teams simply in terms of the increase in the complexity of the environment and technology: "Well, when I joined the company, one engineer could deliver a product or at least the hardware side of it by himself in many cases. But I don't think we'll ever see that again in this company. And it evolved over time to a small group or a well-balanced team of three or four people. At this point, we're looking at twenty-plus people on a project."

In other words, his world is both more technologically complex and more organizationally complex in that the customers are more demanding on multiple dimensions. Meeting these challenges in the context of developing and producing new products is facilitated if the work is organized in teams.

As for what managers actually do as a result of their deeper involvement in teams, it appears that their job has two pieces: managing the internal processes of the teams and acting as an ambassador to other teams. The former involves trying to place the best people on the team, setting priorities, helping the staff deal with problems as they arise, and acting as a general-purpose human resource manager. The latter emerges because as the customer becomes more involved in production, boundaries become unclear and middle management has to negotiate across them. One manager described the internal challenges of working with teams and the set of skills used to address these challenges:

> My challenge is to really make the team bring new talent
> into the team . . . I have taken over a group that just is not
> structured, not on a path to succeed, and I have been
> asked to—myself—take ownership of the problem. And
> the way I have approached it is figuring out where the
> people gaps are. Where there are mismatches in terms
> of what people are doing—where there are ownership
> gaps. So, I have, I guess, a set of tools, mental tools and

processes that I have developed in terms of how I approach that problem.

The second set of skills that teams require is boundary management, an area that is both an opportunity and a challenge. The opportunity comes because the managers who interact with other parts of the organization often gain increased visibility and their careers can be enhanced. I will discuss this in chapter 5. The challenge is that significant and subtle relationship skills are required to successfully engage in boundary work. The challenge, and the solution, was described by a manager in TechCo in just the kind of language that one might find in a course on successful negotiations: "We need to communicate outside a group . . . Making this work, I think, to find the common ground . . . to make sure that we state and understand the business proposition . . . Once we establish that common ground, I think it breaks down a lot of barriers that we can work through. And that has a difficulty in itself because within both organizations, the business proposition isn't always understood."

Not everyone finds boundary management an easy process. As a manager noted, "it requires more relationship skills," and these can be in short supply. One manager expressed this view rather vividly:

> For me personally, it is a major pain in the ass. I don't think that the responsibilities are very clearly defined. And I think, to some extent, that's by design. With my particular group, we have to interface with the software development group, the hardware development group,

and particularly with the other application groups, and there is a slave-and-master relationship that goes on . . . You know, both sides think they're the master, and we decide who wants to be the slave. Somebody has to come in and play Solomon to let them know that they're equal parties here. But I think in most organizations, at least it's been my experience, there's always one organization that thinks they're the superior to the other one. So they're trying to whip it into what they want it to do. Part of my job is to kind of mediate that . . . The top [managers] are not going to want to take on the problem; they want me to solve the problem. But I wouldn't say I'm completely on my own. But it's going to be on me if I don't mediate it. It's me that's going to bear the brunt of it.

Making Trade-Offs

Senior managers, in the language of John Kotter, "set agendas" and, in doing so, shape the direction of the organization.[6] Do middle managers do anything similar? The answer is yes. They make resource-allocation decisions that are central and strategic, though they do so at a lower level and with much less visibility.

In interview after interview, the managers with whom I spoke described their work as mediating between teams and divisions within the organization and between the organization and its customers. An important point is that as organizations have divested themselves of managerial levels, core managerial responsibilities have been pushed down to middle management. Middle managers are now the negotiators between different interests and are making key decisions about trade-offs. One manager commented,

"Everything is important to my boss. So the rest is up to me." Another elaborated: "Now [that] all these issues have come, these trade-offs between quality and timeliness and complexity and all this, who thinks about that in the organization . . . you know, these kinds of decisions and challenges? . . . I think they're mostly dealt with by middle management."

If we look at the older literature on the functions of general managers, then, surprisingly, middle managers start to look very much like the general managers of that literature. Today's middle managers spend a great deal of their time in informal interactions, their day is unplanned, they work across organizational boundaries, and they make choices and trade-offs for their organizations. They are indeed the Chandler's glue that holds the organization together. What has changed is that the organization itself is more complex and diffuse, but this has only increased the importance of managing in the middle.

When I talked to managers about what they did during their days, the description that they gave was consistent with this literature. One manager at TechCo described his day in very much these terms: "And there's a significant portion where it's almost like rain pouring in, where my pager is going off, my phone is going off, and I've got either people from our field organization or just people from other parts of the division asking all these issues to me, like, 'I need your help with this,' 'I need some guidance on this.'"

The nature of the managerial role is not simply that many people and issues are coming at a manager from many directions, but also that the range of the issues that he or she deals with has broadened. Another manager listed what he had to deal with in a given day:

> Let's see, a typical day . . . We have a major initiative this year to sell our latest and hottest brand, and nothing can get in the way of that. So there's a daily meeting to address any issues. And I sit in on that meeting on behalf of my team to try to get a glimpse of what's coming down the pike and what we need to be prepared for in terms of which customers are going to be wanting our product so that we can be prepared from a design standpoint and a material availability standpoint. I'll also, later in the day, run a team meeting where we'll review all the issues at hand with a cross-functional group of managers that report to me and some that don't . . . There's a lot of task forces relative to varying issues or varying marketing activities. I'll have a few one-on-one meetings with my managers to address any particular issue or coaching or things like that—try to make myself available . . . I try to say hello to everybody in the hallway to try to foster a positive esprit de corps. I think that's part of my job as well. From time to time, we'll get on conference calls, which just seem to be more and more of these days with the field teams, the sales and service teams in Europe or in Asia.

What all this adds up to is that managers are running from task to task and are able to give very limited attention to each. Putting out fires might be an exaggeration of what they do, but long-range planning and strategizing would also be an exaggeration. Instead, the role of the middle manager is to grease the wheels of the organization and make it function.

Stress

When middle managers describe their work life, it sounds remarkably similar. They face a variety of challenges—managing their teams, meeting with customers, negotiating at the boundary between their team and others. The intensity is similar: "I find that I have meetings . . . I'd say, about eight hours of meetings. So I'm constantly moving between offices, and that's why I said I carry my network cable in my pocket and my laptop and my notepad. I'm constantly going between meetings."

Middle managers also have the same broad range of relationships that they must manage:

It's a web. For example, I'm going on vacation for the next few weeks, and I'm sending an e-mail . . . to all the people that are basically interacting on a weekly basis, saying please go see such-and-such individual for each particular issue. And I was amazed how long that made up this list. Integrating across peers in the instrumentation group, instrument owners, people on the platform group, people who are responsible for reliability, marketing, senior management. So cutting across all these people, I was really impressed by the size of the list, and then at the end, I concluded that no wonder I'm usually stressed at the end of the day, because I have to deal with all these people and it's demanding.

The starting point of any assessment of how middle managers feel about their work is to recognize that stress has ratcheted up considerably. Certainly, part of this is because of the increased uncertainty that managers face: Will they be able to keep their jobs? But the objective conditions have also changed. Because of the heightened competitive pressure on organizations, more is expected, and because of restructuring, there are fewer people available to deliver. The consequence is stress.

The first source of stress is simply increased hours. Pressure on hours comes from the needs of firms to compete harder in a tougher environment, but in larger measure, it is also due to layoffs, which necessitates that the remaining employees pick up the slack. As one manager in TechCo put it: "But we haven't been able to replace those people, so it's been very hard to get a lot done—treading water in some areas. I think that my boss has relied more on me to pick up more and more, and I think that makes it more stressful. You're almost to a point where you're really being affected if you have all that responsibility. I think we need to rethink that."

A similar point was made by a Bank of America manager: "Every year, there is more pressure, and the worst part of this job is in January, [when] you start off at zero again. You are expected to perform, I mean, whether you are shorthanded or not." Another Bank of America bank manager described how the organization uses technology to keep up the pressure and how people react: "Sometimes it's managed daily . . . The big thing that's changed is the advent of the conference calls. In a typical week, I deal with anywhere from five to eight conference calls . . . People deal with pressure differently . . . The default position is you gradually get beaten down and people start to feel more pressure and more stress."

The second source of stress comes from the uncertainty that managers face regarding their own fate. While on average the vast majority will keep their jobs, some managers, unfortunately, will not. The real probability of a layoff and the haziness of both the layoff process and the layoff criteria introduce considerable uncertainty in the environment. One of the most striking examples was a middle-aged manager in Bank of America who feared not only that people in his group would be fired but also that he was a likely candidate because of his age. His response was to turn to self-help and inspirational books: "So a book like that has, you know, examples of people and things that they have faced and what they have done to be successful, and [the author's] premise is that you don't have to do it. You don't have to actually have a plan in place, but it can evolve over time. There is motivation in [these sorts of books] for me. And . . . although I consider myself fairly well educated, I always learn when I read these books. I kind of get a better idea of what's going on, you know, beyond my vision."

All of this ratchets up the pressure on middle management. The reduction in hierarchical layers means that, in the words of one manager, "the number of people I'm responsible for in different areas has grown." A more vivid description of how the work has changed was provided by a Bank of America manager:

> I mean, five years ago, it was not unusual to work a pretty
> steady forty-hour workweek . . . To me, it was sort of a
> normal expectation for you—typical, you know, let's say

at the time of supervisor-manager. Now, you know, I have a cell phone, which I carry with me everywhere; I have a computer at home, which is pretty much standard for someone in my position. You know, I may only work another ten hours here in the office, probably four nights a week . . . [and am] working from home another hour or two. For me personally, [I work] Saturday mornings, you know, from seven to nine, checking e-mails, and it is not unusual for me to have e-mails waiting from people within the organization, looking for answers on Saturday.

This particular manager thought that the reported productivity gains are in fact deceptive:

I think the job has evolved certainly over the last number of years . . . You certainly have been asked to do more with less; when they talk about efficiencies, you are always here. In other words, the workforce has grown more efficient as the economy has grown at some rate . . . For me as a manager, generally what that means in the real world is that people just work more hours, that they really have not necessarily . . . grown more efficient. Folks are just working more hours for the same pay. So I would say that has been an evolution that has been going on for years, but more so, perhaps in this business for the last four or five.

But regardless of whether people are working better or just harder, stress was a constant theme in my conversations with the managers. And the increased pressure managers feel, when it is combined with the uncertainty induced by the prospect of layoffs, explains the widespread sense that the quality of work has deteriorated.

AUTONOMY AND BREADTH: THE CHANGING WORK OF MIDDLE MANAGERS

While we may have a good, broad understanding of the contours of managerial work, we lack an understanding of how restructuring is changing these contours for middle managers. Are middle managers being squeezed and constrained by the pressures of restructuring, or have they been liberated to be "intrapreneurs" who shape their careers, freed from the limitations of traditional roles and silos? The pop discussion of this question is often one-sided and superficial, but the question is important. Answering it taps into a long-standing social science tradition of trying to understand the content of work and how it is changing. This scholarly interest in the content of work goes at least as far back as Marx, with his description of the "infernal mills" of capitalist factories.

In thinking about the impact of restructuring, we should distinguish between the ideas of autonomy and breadth. Autonomy means the freedom to make decisions about how one does one's work and, sometimes, about the particular tasks to be done. A middle manager with autonomy might be given a set of goals and then have the freedom to figure out how best to achieve these. The idea of breadth is different; it refers to the range of activities that make up a job. How much variety is there in the work, and how wide ranging are the activities? A considerable amount of evidence suggests that employees value both breadth and autonomy.

When it comes to breadth, a long-standing theme in the sociology of work is the fear that the content of people's jobs is increasingly narrowed and de-skilled. The classic example is the skilled machinist who, having learned to shape metal to very fine tolerances, finds his skills rendered obsolete by the emergence of computer-driven machine tools. Or consider the telephone technician who used to arrange wires in complex ways but now simply swaps printed circuit boards into and out of computer frames. What gives this view of the trajectory of work particular bite is the additional argument that top managers want to de-skill work because it gives them more control over their workforce and enables them to hire a cheaper grade of labor. This in turn implies that when management has discretion over what particular technology to adopt and how to implement it, the leaders systematically make choices that de-skill labor.

A great deal of ink has been spilled on both sides of this line of argument. It is not difficult to find particular occupations in which employers appear to be actively de-skilling their workforce. But it is equally easy to find examples that cut the other way. For example, today's automobile assembly line worker no longer resembles Charlie Chaplin's human robot, but instead is more broadly skilled and responsible for quality and process-improvement suggestions and not simply for repeating the same task over and over.[7] If we look at the economy as a whole, the weight of evidence is that demand for skill has increased over time, not declined, as the de-skilling argument implies.[8]

Despite this generally optimistic picture, there are certainly occupations that have been de-skilled and in which top-down control has increased. Has restructuring done this to middle management? The sustained attack on middle management would suggest that it is an occupation whose autonomy has been systematically constrained. The question about whether work has become narrower and more controlled is not applicable to senior executives and seems simply out of context. On the other hand, the question does make sense for middle managers, because in some significant way, these managers can be considered workers who are acted on by the organization.

For some managers, restructuring has led to jobs that are, simply put, narrower. The range of tasks that they engage in is more limited and constrained than in the past. Recall that Nancy from chapter 1 complained that her job had been "blown apart" and that Robert the information technology manager found himself under the thumb of the "dreaded metrics." Another manager who ran a technical operation within the bank described it this way: "Yes, well, it has changed over the years a bit. There was technology in operations, and I used to work two halves a bit more than I do today. I used to be involved in a lot of other technology-related projects, offer implementation conversions. As we grew, my field of expertise became narrower. You know, it becomes more difficult to be jack-of-all-trades. That means two hundred trades, you know, two hundred years of expertise."

This manager regretted what had happened but had no choice: "For me personally, I would have rather remained in a more broad world within the group, that is, where some of my interests lie, learning new projects, working with different people, learning new products and the skills that come along with, you know, what is required to do that work . . . [The decision] was very much given to me."

It would be easy to conclude from these examples, and from the compelling rhetoric of the de-skilling story, that middle-management jobs are being narrowed and autonomy is being eliminated. Some middle managers, however, do not feel that their autonomy is being squeezed or that their work is getting narrower. For example, as previously described in this chapter, Mary, one of the most successful lending managers at Bank of America, found an increase in autonomy as the reorganizations led to her superior's paying less attention to her.

A branch manager at Bank of America also felt that over time, his job was increasing in breadth:

I think the job is becoming much broader over time. As a manager, in the past, you were an order taker. You know, it's a very reactive business; people didn't have direct deposit or home link or electronic banking to the extent they have it now, so a lot of them went through their lobby, and there are plenty of opportunities to do trans-actions and just react to what was in front of you. Over time, the job entailed much more outreach and coordi-nation of outreach. We are in a mature market in New England, and therefore, the person that goes and gets it is the one who's going to have it. They introduced special-ists into our world, so not only was I managing tellers and platform folks, but now I had to be able to manage specialists, investment specialists, business specialists, operational specialists, people that are in exempt status. So [it's] an upgrade of the level of professionals working for you. Therefore, as a manager, you needed to adapt your approach. Another thing you needed to do was [that] you were evaluated on your ability to produce good specialists.

Chimneys

While for many managers the jobs have in fact broadened, the pop version of "intrapreneurialism" does not find much support. One of the conceits of writers who believe that middle managers have been liberated by a restructuring is the claim that the organizational chimneys of old have been shattered and that the newly liberated managers can move across functional areas as they construct their careers. Certainly, functional chimneys did characterize the old organizations. A study of careers at AT&T in the 1950s and 1960s found that virtually no one moved across departments.[9] In his broader sample of managers in the 1970s, David Granick reported a great deal of job changing, with only 20 percent of his managers staying for more than three years in one position but with very few (18 percent) moving across functional areas.[10] Has this changed?

There are two ways of thinking about this question. One is to ask whether people move across chimneys. At Bank of America, this might mean starting off in lending to middle-size firms and then moving into personal wealth management for individuals. At TechCo, it might mean switching between the groups that are responsible for product design and those responsible for manufacturing or sales. The second angle on the topic is to ask whether people substantially broaden or change their skill sets over time even if they stay in the same broad functional area.

At both Bank of America and TechCo, moving across functional areas, that is, across chimneys, is very rare. At TechCo, one manager commented, "I think most people tend to stay within their division, their silo of expertise . . . There are some people who transition into different spots, but I don't think that is the norm." At Bank of America, only one middle manager whom I interviewed, a branch manager who moved into wealth management, changed silos over the course of his career.

While people do spend their careers within chimneys, many managers have been aggressive in adding to their skill set and getting involved in new activities. This was particularly noticeable at TechCo, where the project team model of doing the work encourages skill broadening because the regular breakup of teams forces the members to search for new work, which often involves new repertoires. As an example, the same manager who commented that people stay within silos has moved from managing the firm's TQM processes, to managing the testing of the product prior to shipping to customers, to learning project management skills (and getting a certificate in this), to running the group responsible for tracking projects as they progress. Another TechCo manager who has spent his career within the same functional area nonetheless saw some movement: "I would say I probably moved in some redefinition of my role every two or three years."

Autonomy

Autonomy is the obverse of control; we cannot talk about one without bringing in the other. A central role of management, at any level, is to exercise control over the activities of the members of the organization. The problem is complicated by what economists term the principal-agent problem. Principal-agent problems arise when there is a divergence between the objectives of the boss and those of a subordinate. For example, the dean may want me to devote a large fraction of my time to being an excellent teacher, but I prefer to focus on my research and writing. One solution is to create an extensive monitoring and control system to manage my behavior. In some sense, this is what the traditional hierarchy tried to do with its "checkers watching the checkers." Another approach, and sometimes a more effective and less costly one, is to create a compensation system (broadly defined to include both pay and promotions) that seeks to align my incentives with those of my boss. For example, a large portion of my pay might be based on student evaluations. Of course—and this fact of life is often overlooked—any such system can be subverted, and in the end, checkers may still be needed. I might, say, figure out that the way to get good evaluations is to teach a "gut" course and give uniformly high grades. In any case, there is a strong drive to use incentives instead of bureaucracy to align behaviors within organizations.

The need for control has not disappeared with restructuring, but restructuring brings with it new techniques, some of which may be more appealing than the ham-handed monitoring of the checkers and the heavy layers of bureaucracy. One such strategy is greater use of information technology, a strategy that is central to reengineering. An example is provided by Harland Prechel's description of changes in a large steel firm.[11] In his pseudonymous Target Steel, middle managers had, prior to the restructuring, substantial control over the organization and operation of the individual steel mills in which they worked. The complexity of the numerous product lines as well as the technical variability in the steelmaking process meant that corporate management was unable to establish formal control systems and had to rely on the "personal cooperation among middle managers" to make the system work. To the extent that corporate management maintained control, it was via the budget and not the management of day-to-day activities.

Under the old regime, middle managers were responsible for quality, but the tendency was to let quality slip and to hope that responsibility for defects would fall on downstream units. This was no longer acceptable in the more difficult, competitive environment. In response, new systems such as statistical process control were implemented, the firm pushed toward a "one best way" to manufacture each product, and the company established an "operations control center" to use information technology to monitor production throughout the entire corporation. In the words of one manager, "these controls take the humanistic element out of the decision-making process." Another manager commented that "middle managers used to be the people that provided the information . . . With the increase in information technology, . . . they are no longer the information sources."

In this example, the managers felt hemmed in and experienced a loss of autonomy. But this need not always be the case. In fact, it is helpful to think about scope and control at two levels: the larger system and constraints within which managers work, and the day-to-day activities of their jobs. Middle managers are being increasingly hemmed in by decisions not of their making. The decisions regarding the shape of the enterprise—what is in and what is out—as well as the size in term of both layoffs and the number of levels are simply outside the realm of middle management. This has always been true, of course, but in the past, the nature of the firm was stable, whereas today it is constantly being reconsidered and reshaped. The continuous organizational turmoil that ensues creates an environment that seems chaotic and out of control from the perspective of middle management.

Many of the managers interviewed in Bank of America felt that their work was becoming increasingly controlled. Perhaps the most remarkable example is the stories told by the managers of local bank branches. Recall that the branch manager quoted earlier felt that his job was getting broader. But breadth—the range of skills required—is not the same as control, and for branch managers, control is disappearing. Up until the takeover, bank branch managers were measured by the volume and profitability of their branch and by their ability to sell banking products. How people did this was their own business, and they were encouraged to be creative: "We had a lot of autonomy," said one manager. "You were pretty much on your own until you needed help or someone showed up every quarter or every year." The situation today is very different. Branch managers are required to stand in the lobby greeting customers, are given "seven priorities and fifty goals," and have to fill out daily report sheets showing how they have done on these measures. Their workday is totally scripted by headquarters. They are not judged simply on results as before, but also on process, and the process is heavily controlled. The managers have clear views on this: "I am frustrated because [despite] these skills that I brought to the job, sales and management skills and being able to achieve goals, I lose the freedom to determine how I get there."

In making these changes, the bank is driven by the example of large retailers, such as Wal-Mart, that try to create a common experience for customers across all locations. Indeed, outside senior managers in Bank of America have been hired precisely from these retailers.

At TechCo, control is exercised less through checklists than via the strong organizational culture, a culture that virtually all managers termed "fault oriented." The style of interaction among managers is to identify problems and pound on them. A typical description of the culture was provided by one manager:

> There's a weakness-focused management style . . . Generally, managers poke at the gaps, poke at the short-comings, poke at the deficiencies, and they end up, if you have a two-hour meeting, you end up talking about all negative stuff. And as the guys were walking out of the room [they'll say], "Oh, by the way, you did a great job!" One of the former executives of this company was interviewing a financial manager and said, "Oh, by the way, how do you respond to positive feedback? Is that something that you need in order to succeed in your job and to be content with your position? Because if so, you aren't gonna get it here."

An even more extreme version of this point was provided by another manager: "This is the shouting, yeah. It is considered acceptable in some meetings, at least with some managers I've had opportunity to interact with. They seem to think it's acceptable to go into a meeting in a public forum, criticize someone's work on a level which I think is really inappropriate. There's a difference between pointing out the fact that, yeah, they screwed up, but you don't go in there and belittle them in front of a large crowd."

The point is that the informal culture of the organization pushes hard against people's taking too many risks, because the price of failure is high. A great deal of research has convincingly demonstrated that the informal culture of an organization can override formal objectives. In the case of TechCo, efforts to think or act too far outside the box may be encouraged in principle but are often punished in practice.

PATTERNS IN THE NATIONAL DATA

Understanding how work has changed is in some respects better done through fieldwork than through survey research. Surveys cannot capture the texture of what actually happens on the job. Furthermore, in surveys, people often give what they perceive as the socially expected answers to questions. How else, as many scholars have noted, can we understand the high rates of job satisfaction reported to survey researchers by people in the worst-paying, least prestigious, and most unpleasant jobs? Nonetheless, it may be useful to compare what the managerial interviews tell us about the trajectory of work with what the survey researchers have to say. The Quality of Employment Survey (1977) and the National Study of the Changing Workforce (1997 and 2002) asked the same questions about autonomy and

TABLE 4-1

Self-reported sense of job autonomy and control for managers and other workers, 1977 and 2002

	MANAGERS (% RESPONDING YES)		NONMANAGERS (% RESPONDING YES)	
	1977	2002	1977	2002
AUTONOMY				
I keep learning on the job.	63	71	36	59
The job lets me use skills.	45	76	24	67
The job lets me be creative.	41	62	33	41
I decide how to do the job.	42	65	26	54
CONTROL				
I have freedom to decide what to do.	28	38	14	24
I have a lot of say about what happens on the job.	37	53	17	29

Source: Data from Families and Work Institute, *National Study of the Changing Workforce*, surveys 1997 and 2002 (New York: Families and Work Institute, 1997 and 2002), available at Cornell Institute for Social and Economic Research Web page, http://www.ciser.cornell.edu/ASPs/search_athena.asp?CODEBOOK=SIND-026&IDTITLE=2104; and U.S. Department of Labor, *Quality of Employment Survey* (Ann Arbor: University of Michigan, 1977).

control. Table 4-1 groups the questions into two broad categories. The first category—autonomy—measures the extent to which people have opportunities to use their skills and to learn new ones; it represents the degree to which people can expand their capabilities, both for the current job and for any future ones. The second category—control—is about voice and power, yet another dimension that is central for quality jobs. Numerous surveys demonstrate that employees, regardless of their union status, want to have an opportunity to participate in workplace decisions and to exercise control over how they do their work.

Presumably, this is even more true for managers, who are trained to make decisions, than for other employees.

The table shows the percentage of managers who strongly agree with the statements about their job, and it compares the responses from the two surveys. To provide some perspective, the data are also presented for nonmanagerial employees.

The overall patterns in the data are striking. The jobs held by these managers are rich in opportunities to learn and in autonomy over how the job itself is done. But the power of managers to control the overall nature of their work or the context in which they operate is much more modest. Perhaps most surprising, on both dimensions the circumstances of managers improved over the more-than-twenty-year period represented in the data. Restructuring is changing the nature of managerial work, but, as I noted earlier, not always in a negative direction.

Compared with managers, other employees clearly have jobs with on average less opportunity for learning and creativity and less control. However, the rate at which their jobs improved was in fact faster than the rate for managers. Put differently, there has been a substantial degree of convergence between the nature of managerial work and other jobs. This convergence almost certainly reflects the spread of teams, quality programs, and other aspects of high-commitment work systems.

CONCLUSION

Middle managers get the organization's job done. Much of their day-to-day work comprises the ordinary tasks that, taken together, add up to what their firm is about. These tasks, however, can also be thought of as the more general functions that cut across any particular functional responsibility. Middle managers are the communication conduits within organizations. As teams have become more important, middle managers, on the one hand, hold the teams together internally and, on the other, play ambassadorial roles across teams. Because firms have reduced layers and cut back on staffing, the stress level of middle managers has risen as they are required to take on more responsibilities. And because of fewer layers between them and the top and because of the diffusion of information technology, middle managers are faced with more monitoring and control than in the past. For the same set of reasons, however, their jobs are broader and more complex. Not only do middle managers do more than they did before, but they also find themselves making the kinds of trade-offs and allocational decisions conventionally considered the domain of those at the top. The not surprising consequence is that stress levels are up sharply.

The restructuring that has remade the content of middle management work has also rewritten the expectations for advancement and the pathways of careers. This is an additional source of confusion and stress for middle managers and is the topic of chapter 5.

Careers in the Middle

Climbing the Ladder or Not

In the office in which I work there are five people of whom I am afraid. Each of these five people is afraid of four people (excluding overlaps), for a total of twenty, and each of these twenty people is afraid of six people, making a total of one hundred and twenty people who are feared by at least one person. Each of these one hundred and twenty people is afraid of the other one hundred and nineteen, and all of these one hundred and forty-five people are afraid of the twelve men at the top.

—Bob Slocum in Joseph Heller's *Something Happened*

The Corporation is a pyramid of opportunity.

—Alfred P. Sloan, *Adventures of a White Collar Man*

Bob Slocum is a figment of Joseph Heller's imagination, and Alfred P. Sloan was the very real founder of General Motors and one of the architects of the modern corporation. Slocum's and Sloan's differences aside, their thoughts capture two live and actively vying perspectives on the circumstances of managers trying to climb the corporate ladder. In a vote, the odds today would be on Slocum's take on reality, but this was not always true. In her study of a large industrial firm some thirty years ago, Rosabeth Kanter observed that "it was hard for success to mean anything else but movement."[1] Moving up and attaining power was the only important goal for managers and was topmost on everyone's minds.

Kanter is not alone in her characterization of corporate America. In his ethnography of corporate life, Robert Jackell writes about the importance of movement: "Striving for success is, of course, a moral imperative in American society. In the corporate world this means moving up or getting ahead in the organization . . . even standing still for an instant, symbolically or actually, can be dangerous."[2] Some managers come out on top in this competition and others fail, but Jackell believes that all managers are victims in that they have in some important sense lost their soul or their integrity in playing the game. "At the psychological level, managers have an acute sense of organizational contingency."[3] Of course, even in Jackell's deeply cynical world, not every manager is a player, but those who opt out (because they might care about family or other activities or because they feel that they cannot win) are, in Jackell's view, "drones" or "highly paid clerks."[4]

The imagery utilized by economists is much less vivid and their prose much thinner, but their idea is the same: the goal of employees is to gain promotions and to increase their wages.

Indeed, getting ahead and making more money are, in the economists' view, the fundamental motivation of all employees.

If moving up is the sine qua non of success, consider the challenge facing "Steve," a midlevel manager, at TechCo. Steve seems the perfect candidate to climb the corporate ladder. A mechanical engineer who went on to get an MBA, he loves his work: "Personally, I'm somewhat of a workaholic." In fact, he attributes the collapse of his first marriage to his work habits and describes a typical day as "seven to seven . . . If I get out of here by seven, I feel pretty good . . . because [of] the time I am willing to spend to make sure I understand the business at a high level."

Steve is responsible for dealing with TechCo's suppliers and for assuring that their product meets all specifications and quality standards. This is the third or fourth job he has held in the firm, and up until now, he felt that he was on an upward trajectory. He still feels (perhaps naively) that the business itself is good, but when asked about his future prospects and the chances for moving up the ladder, he becomes uncertain:

> I've kind of struggled with that question in terms of
> what's next or what am I aspiring to . . . It used to be,
> I think, as the company grew . . . [there were] lots of
> opportunities. Now I think we're on a much more oscil-
> lating environment that those opportunities won't pre-
> sent themselves as readily. Would I be content being called
> a midlevel manager? . . . Absolutely. I would not have a
> problem with that as long as the work was good. As soon
> as I think I have stopped learning and I kind of see it

happening—it happens to individuals where essentially their skill set tends to look like it's a mismatch in terms of what the company needs—and I am not able to meet those limits, then I'm probably going to look elsewhere.

Steve is confronting a common issue for middle managers today: both the opportunities and rules for advancement have changed. Much the same is true for Robert, the information technology manager we met at the beginning of chapter 4. He thinks that he could fill his boss's job, but he may never get it. And his subordinates are in the same fix: "Many people are fixed on the traditional hierarchy. 'Show me the roadmap.' That may have worked twenty years ago with fixed technology and slow organizational change, but career planning today is 'OK, what are you going to do in the next six months?' I can't imagine sitting down with someone and saying, 'What are you going to do in three years?'"

A different set of career problems confront "Marsha," a human resources manager in her fifties and a TechCo lifer. In keeping with the general tenor of all conversations with HR people in both Bank of America and TechCo, she has a somewhat jaundiced and cynical view of who does well and who does not in her organization. But when it comes to gender issues, her restrained sense of irony takes a harsher tone.

The conversation began with the broad theme of why relatively few (roughly 11 percent) of the firm's managers are women. Her first explanation was the organization's culture:

And so they [top management] are less inclined to be, I think, sensitive and respectful in understanding cultural

differences or gender differences. Sometimes it astounds
me. I had struck up a conversation with someone about
why in a group of sixty people that worked for him, there
was not a single woman. He goes back and tells somebody else, "She wants me to hire more girls." . . . And he
was a fairly young guy. And I am like, "What am I going
to do with him?" . . . It's just that it somehow feels like
they don't come up for air to see the world around them,
to notice. They don't notice. And so then, when you
point it out to them, they are like. . . . It's either like, "OK,
I'll listen to this woman for as long as she is talking, to get
out the door," or they are looking kind of bewildered.

Another factor, which Marsha acknowledged, is the relative
dearth of women who study computer science in universities.
This has been of some concern at MIT, for example. Overall,
however, Marsha attributed the problem to the clueless and
often harsh and aggressive culture at TechCo. Then, as the conversation evolved, we turned to her own career, and Marsha's
affect of ironic weariness turned to anger. A boss had once called
her too aggressive and ambitious, and this grated, but the real
grievance came when an international posting opened up and it
went to someone else. "So I go to the guy who decided—the boss
at the time—and I said, 'Was I even considered for that position?' And he looked at me and said no. And I said, 'Why was
that?' [He replied] 'Oh, I didn't realize that you would want to be
considered. We didn't think about it.'"

Of course, how much people—both men and women—
actually care about getting ahead and what trade-offs they are

willing to make, or not to make, is more complex than might be assumed. We will see that a great many middle managers are in fact not aggressive players in the ladder-climbing game. Nevertheless, the career patterns of managers are of central concern, both to the managers and to anyone else trying to understand their world.

DRIVING SUCCESS

As I observed in chapter 2, during the heyday of the "organization man" there was, as the popular image suggests, stable, long-term employment, although there was also more turnover than the stereotype would imply. The career patterns themselves were relatively simple and straightforward, with movement up well-defined ladders housed in functional chimneys being the norm. Upward mobility was a reasonable expectation for many managers. Today, as we will see, the process is more problematic. But we should begin by asking whether upward mobility remains the central goal of today's middle managers.

Who Wants to Move Up?

Standard thinking assumes that everyone wants to get ahead, but there is in fact considerable variability about who wants to advance and who does not. This does not deny that some middle managers are ambitious and competitive. One bank branch manager, who had weekly conference calls with colleagues who managed branches elsewhere in his region, spoke of "crushing those guys like bugs." About a third of the managers I spoke with in TechCo were interested in moving up in the organization.

Many of these managers found themselves confused by the frequent reorganizations, and my interviews with these people revealed that the managers devoted time to scanning their environment, trying to discern the appropriate pathways and the right strategies to follow to get ahead.

But if a minority of the managers were eager to advance, the majority were not. In part this was due to obvious life-cycle issues: after a certain age, the internal fire is dampened. As one fifty-four-year-old bank manager put it:

> It sort of depends on where you are in your career cycle, and I'm done conquering the world, as far as I'm concerned at this point. I'm older in my life . . . I'm still pushing myself to make or exceed whatever goals I have to the extent that I can, but I don't have to be number one anymore . . . Yeah, I think I've done a fair amount in my career, and to do what I've done in banking. And in the other stuff, I think that I can give that to other folks to, hopefully, sort of model . . . I can spread myself out more. There's a lot of satisfaction; I can still feel a lot of satisfaction.

A second restraint on ambition is that people who see that they are unlikely to rise much further adapt by changing their expectations. This is similar to what the AT&T researchers found in that classic "old style" corporation half a century ago—a corporation that was replicated twenty years later by Kanter.[5] Over time, the young managers who were more successful became more involved in work, and the less successful ones became more involved in family, church, and recreation. In some sense, the latter group gave up. At AT&T, these differences did not show up at the initial interviews, so it does not appear that one group was intrinsically less ambitious than the other. The explanation is straightforward: as people learn that they are not destined for great things, they adjust their interests.

A TechCo manager who has chosen to spend more time coaching his children than tending to his career is self-aware about this process:

> I have made . . . a conscious decision to leave work
> around five o'clock. I try to get on the four-fifty bus just
> about every day. That all started to coincide with the
> start of T-ball season, so my son, who is five years old . . .
> my wife volunteered us to coach his team. So I was
> spending two days a week teaching five-year-old kids
> how to play T-ball, and so, that coincided with a certain
> toning down, a certain prioritization. So I think, maybe . . .
> I don't know that I can see that I've forgone anything
> because of that, but I certainly made a conscious choice
> there. I was going to get done what I could get done in
> that time frame . . . And would I have made that choice if
> I were on a meteoric ascension? A path of meteoric
> ascension? Probably not.

It is not only middle-aged managers or slow movers who have limited ambition. Nancy, whom we met in chapter 1, has no husband or children at home and is clearly successful, yet she too has set some limits on her professional aspirations: "The reality is I have worked too hard to get balance in my life, and I don't want to give it up. I don't want to ruin my life. If it means working a few more years longer . . . I try and keep my tennis up, and I've been taking piano lessons and doing all that stuff."

An additional reason some managers do not want to advance is risk aversion. People perceive that upward mobility increases vulnerability. A manager at Bank of America made this point sharply:

> In knowing what I know [about] what happened when
> Bank of America and Nations Bank merged and then
> with this Fleet merger, I've noticed that the further up
> you get, and the further away from eye contact with the
> customer, the more at risk you become as far as layoffs
> and everything. That's just the way it is. And I've also rec-
> ognized that . . . at this point, I can pretty much control a
> lot of things that I wouldn't be able to control at a larger
> level . . . What I've noticed is that when it's time to make
> a change, and you may have somebody that may not be
> getting the type of production that they need, what I've
> noticed is that the first person that they move are those
> middle managers.

The National Study of the Changing Workforce (1997 and 2002) asked people what level of responsibility they hoped to achieve in their jobs: more, the same, or less. The responses to this question among managers are shown in table 5-1, which contains both the overall response and the response by age.

Apparently, there is considerable dispersion in managers' desire to attain more responsibility. The patterns of responses also reflect what common sense would predict: people who think that their prospects are good are likely to want to move up,

TABLE 5-1

Preferences for degree of responsibility among managers

Level of responsibility desired	ALL AGES (%)		AGED 45 OR YOUNGER (%)	
	All	High expectations*	All	High expectations*
Want more	44	48	50	52
Want the same	45	44	38	39
Want less	11	7	12	8

Source: Data from Families and Work Institute, *National Study of the Changing Workforce*, surveys 1997 and 2002 (New York: Families and Work Institute, 1997 and 2002), available at Cornell Institute for Social and Economic Research Web page, http://www.ciser.cornell.edu/ASPs/search_athena.asp?CODEBOOK=SIND-026&IDTITLE=2104.

* *High expectations* refers to managers who think their chances of advancement are excellent or good.

and younger people are more ambitious than older. However, it is also apparent that more is at play than frustrated or plateaued people giving in to the facts of life. Even among young managers who rate their chances of advancement as good, only barely over half want more responsibility in their future work. The assumption of ambition that drives much of the economics literature regarding motivation and how to incentivize people appears to apply to only a subset of managers.

Gender

Are there differences between men and women managers in their desire to move up or in their commitment to work? And if there are such differences, where do they come from? Both my interviews and the national data show that women managers are deeply committed to their jobs and work full-time. There are, however, differences on the margin between the genders, and the differences come from work-versus-family conflicts.

When the answers to the question about desire to advance are broken out by gender, 49 percent of the male managers said that they hoped to attain jobs with more responsibility, while only 36 percent of the women managers expressed this sentiment. By contrast, 7 percent of the male managers said that they hoped that their responsibility would diminish over time, while 15 percent of the women managers did so (the balance of both groups wanted to maintain the same level). While many male and female managers share the same aspirations, more women than men apparently have what might be termed limited aspirations. This pattern is consistent with a body of research that shows that men are more willing than women to enter competitions, even when the ability to succeed is the same. In one such experiment, researchers devised a simple task that both genders did equally well and offered participants the choice of two compensation schemes: a simple piece rate or compensation based on how the person did in a contest or tournament. A notably higher percentage of the men chose the tournament, even though they were no better than the women at the actual task.[6]

Some of the women I spoke to recognized this pattern. "Heather" is a successful player at Bank of America. In her mid-forties with a husband who was back in graduate school, Heather had managed to come out on top in the merger. She had improved her position and had done so by aggressively getting in front of the new Bank of America masters by sending them memos with her ideas regarding the reorganization. Nonetheless, she saw a clear difference between the behavior of men and women in the organization:

> But your typical male employee gets that new job, and [on] day one, he is worrying about "How do I position myself for the next new job?" Your typical female employee gets a new job, and all she cares about is doing a really good job and doing the best with that job and does not think about the next opportunity. The female stays in that same position for a longer period of time and gets pigeonholed, and [there is] the feeling that she does well but I do not know if she can do something else, whereas the guy is, like, always moving on to the next piece.

Heather attributes the "ambition gap" to an intrinsic gender difference, but a more situational explanation lies in work and family realities. Another woman manager at Bank of America described her job as follows: "There's not a lot of room for creativity, which on the one hand, I don't like, but I don't have a lot of brainpower for creativity right now. As the mother of three who's just got a lot going on, if we get through those tasks in a year, that's a good year, and I get paid well to do that, that's not so bad."

Surveys are a crude way to get at these distinctions, but I can ask whether single women without children have higher aspirations than those set by married women with children. Table 5-2 shows the distribution of preferences for two groups of men and women: single people with no children and married people with children.

TABLE 5-2

Preferences for degree of responsibility among men and women managers

Level of responsibility desired	SINGLE, NO CHILDREN (%)		MARRIED WITH CHILDREN (%)	
	Men	Women	Men	Women
Want more	51.0	43.9	58.7	31.5
Want less	9.2	10.3	4.0	14.6

Source: Data from Families and Work Institute, *National Study of the Changing Workforce*, surveys 1997 and 2002 (New York: Families and Work Institute, 1997 and 2002), available at Cornell Institute for Social and Economic Research Web page, http://www.ciser.cornell.edu/ASPs/search_athena.asp?CODEBOOK=SIND-026&IDTITLE=2104.

It is clear that family status makes a considerable difference. In addition, the impact on men and women is in opposite directions: being married and having children reduces women's work ambitions, while it increases men's. But even among single, childless people, women are somewhat less ambitious than men, though the gap is relatively modest. This points us directly toward work-versus-family issues as a central driver in understanding the dynamics of work for women managers. To a large extent, the "ambition gap" is due to work-versus-family constraints and cross-pressures that confront women far more than these pressures affect men.

While there are gender differences in the "incidence of ambition," a substantial number of both men and women do want to rise in their organizations. Women, as Marsha made clear earlier in this chapter, face challenges beyond those that confront their male colleagues. But for both genders, the rules have changed, a topic I turn to now.

THE NEW RULES

If the old AT&T represented the essence of the old system of managerial careers, consider what has happened to the company's vaunted career-planning system that I described earlier. The firm itself was battered by the breakup of its monopoly and the rise of numerous telecommunications competitors. All this rendered extremely difficult the kind of employment forecasting that lay behind the managerial development system. And that system died. Peter Cappelli quotes a consultant who worked under the old regime and who was asked to return to help design a new one: "I was in the same building I had been in before, the appraisal unit was completely gone, and the new HR people in the building weren't even aware that the company ever had an appraisal unit."[7]

Some popular discussions assume that career systems for managers have been totally blown apart and all that remains is a new free market in which insiders and outsiders compete on an equal footing for a diminishing number of secure jobs. This picture would be a gross exaggeration. Overall, managerial employment has more than held its own in recent decades, and even in the "good old days," there was a substantial degree of turnover and outside hiring at all levels in the managerial ranks. Nor does the inability to engage in the kind of massive planning and development that characterized the old AT&T mean that stable managerial careers have disappeared. Nonetheless, any conversation with middle managers makes it clear that, as C. Wright Mills said in another context, the "tang and feel" of managerial careers have changed. We see these shifts in Bank of America, which remains a more traditionally structured organization with clear functional chimneys, and in TechCo, which is a more "modern" firm that makes great use of project teams and in which the lines of progression are much less clear. The data also support pessimism. In the National Study of the Changing Workforce, only a third of managers strongly agreed with the proposition that their chances of advancement were good.

In thinking about how restructuring has affected career patterns, two channels stand out. First, assessment, while always difficult, has been made harder because of the nature of the new jobs and the instability among supervisors. Second, traditional pathways have been disrupted, and because of slow growth and the loss of rungs on the ladder, there are fewer opportunities to move up.

Difficult Assessment

Under the best of circumstances, managerial assessment is a difficult business. One problem is that middle managers typically work in groups and do not produce an easily measurable product. More worrisome is that middle managers are asked to do many different tasks, whose relative weights are not always clear.

Some managers believe that performance measures are so weak that the assessments are relatively easy to manipulate, as one of my interviewees explained: "I do think there is a level of performance, but I can manipulate it. My level of performance that I am rewarded for is not something that I would necessarily say is where I should be, and they think that I'm pretty terrific partly because my client thought I was great. Well great, I pulled the wool over my client's eyes . . . There's lots of other people who probably don't think I'm terrific, but nobody is going to ask them. I can manipulate the perceptions of myself."

Most managers are not this cynical. But the deeper issue is that much of what they do is relatively invisible and hard to capture in clean measures. Even for commercial loans, the banking managers I spoke with believed that accurate metrics of their productivity were hard to gather and that it was hard to know what led to success: "That's always a good question. I think my stuff is much more subjective versus, 'How many loans did I close today, how much dollar revenue did I bring in?' My job is more, 'How much have I saved? Have I prevented losses?'" Another manager, this time in TechCo, made a similar point: "As an example, an area that I put a lot of energy into is recruiting good people, team building, and retaining talent, and there is very little recognition of that in the fairly simple metrics that you can generate."

The second difficulty is that when performance metrics are used, they are unreliable. An early critique of these measures came from a study of the relationship between experience, earnings, and performance among managerial employees in two American corporations in the late 1970s.[8] The two economists conducting the study found that while earnings rose with experience (i.e., time on the job), there was no such relationship between experience and performance, as measured by the two firms' performance evaluation systems. In other words, the outcome of importance to the managers—their earnings trajectory—seemed unaffected by the performance evaluations that they received. A leading personnel psychology textbook explains why this happens: the relationship between performance evaluations done at one time and actual performance over time gets progressively weaker as time passes. That is, performance evaluation measures are unreliable.[9]

Even if performance was visible and if metrics were clear, the disruption caused by restructuring introduces a great deal of noise into performance evaluation. People's supervisors keep changing, and as a result, relationships and understandings are hard to build, as one interviewee explained: "The people who I report to and who determine my reward have not been around long enough to build a relationship with me. The first year, I had one supervisor; the second year, I have another." Another manager captured all these problems:

> Also, you have one relationship with one senior manager and figure out the value structure and communication scheme, that could change overnight . . . So that's literally what happened in this case. I worked for one gentleman . . . We had a very high level [of] communication; we had similar values. It was very clear what his goals were; they resonated with my goals, and it was really progressing to the point where I would have thought the next few steps were relatively obvious and becoming available. Over the course of just a few months, the whole organization changed, and I myself [was] reporting to a different vice president. He's about a hundred eighty degrees different than my former one. Now I'm struggling to learn what his values are. The communication and the alignment is much less obvious.

In short, the traditional rules for getting ahead are in doubt. Job paths are no longer clear, networks are disrupted, and the metrics for performance assessment and the criteria for judging who gets ahead are confused. Asked how to get ahead, one TechCo manager's answer was both simple and representative: "I don't know. I really don't know."

Women and the Politics of Advancement

Getting ahead in organizations certainly depends to an important degree on merit, but playing the political game is also important. Robert Jackell takes an extreme, but not entirely inaccurate, view: "What matters in the bureaucratic world is not what a person is but how well his many persona mesh with the organizational ideal; not his willingness to stand by his actions but his agility in avoiding blame . . . not his talents, abilities, or his hard work . . . not what he stands for but whom he stands with."[10]

One of the themes that constantly emerged in my interviews was that the women middle managers felt uncomfortable playing this political game. In fact, a good deal of research supports the idea that women have more difficulty than men in navigating political waters at work. A well-known body of research by Linda Babcock and her colleagues shows that women are less likely to negotiate for themselves at work, and "as a result, women in business often watch their male colleagues pull ahead, receive better assignments, get promoted more quickly, and earn more money."[11] More than negotiations are at play here, however. The women managers with whom I talked also felt uncomfortable with other aspects of office politics, for example, the maneuvering needed to make contacts and develop an "old boys" network.

Mary, the highly successful lending manager described in chapter 4, manages a large group in the mortgage division of the bank. She likes her work and finds it stimulating: "It changes all the time, and there are always people trying to come up with and cook up different and better ways to do things." She has a stay-at-home husband, and her children are well past elementary school age, so the path is mostly clear for her. And while she is in a responsible position, she notes that "I would like to move up." The problem is the politics: "Yeah, there is a certain amount of politics. I don't think I am particularly good at it. So, I think it's probably why I do not like it. We never like anything we are not good at, probably . . . That's not a skill that I have learned well . . . I wished I could. Sometimes I feel like . . . you are on the stand . . . Your honesty and your valued input is not only always the thing that they are looking for first—not always." What really bothers Mary is that she thinks that her discomfort with politics has hurt her because "it can get more difficult to be recognized for the achievements that you have versus having said the right thing."

These kinds of sentiments were echoed in most of my interviews with women managers. For example, another woman loan officer in the community services part of the bank felt pressure to make suboptimal loans for political reasons. She was willing to do this, but feared that she would be blamed if the loans underperformed. Her problem was that she did not know how to manage this situation: "I tend to be too honest." I asked her if being a woman made it harder to play this critical game. "Sometimes," she answered. "I hate to hide behind this, but yes."

The discomfort that the women managers feel about playing the political game may have something to do with their upbringing. But it may also reflect an accurate assessment that women in organizations pay a higher price than do men for being aggressive and self-assertive. Some social psychology literature compares people's reactions to both men and women who are self-promoters, and the reactions are quite different. A recent review summarized the findings: "Speaking directly and high-lighting one's accomplishments can make a woman less likeable, attractive, and hirable as a partner for a competitive game, whereas self-promoting men do not suffer these costs."[12]

The difficulty of politics merges with the challenge of fitting in. Indeed, the problems with fitting in were the main theme of Kanter's classic book *Men and Women of the Corporation*. Her argument was that women's advancement is blocked because the dominant workgroup (men) prefers to interact with people like themselves. Communication is easier, it is possible to talk in shorthand, and the level of implicit trust is higher. As a result, the structure replicates itself. This pattern certainly was consistent with the observations of "Leslie," a manager at Bank of America: "I can tell you that working with seven guys who are sitting at your desk and really no diversity—I will not put myself in that position again . . . The conversation outside of markets is sports-oriented or, you know, going-out-and-drinking-oriented . . . You know, guys without families—I do not blame them for having no interest in what my three-year-old said or did; it is just a nat-ural human thing. Men are from Mars, women are from Venus, and that separates [the two groups] when you are not talking about the market."

This kind of mismatch may seem trivial in that it only leads to boring lunch conversations. But in fact there is more at stake. In talking about mentors, one woman manager commented, "If I were to think about it . . . I would be more comfortable having a conversation with another woman than I would a colleague that's male." The numerical distribution of men and women managers and the extent to which women managers feel able to find someone that they can connect to has real consequences for career patterns.

Broken Ladders and Disrupted Pathways

In the old regime, the pathways were stable and predictable over many years. Managers knew that the way to get to job B was to first hold job A and that job B was the entry point to job C. As discussed in chapter 2, this stability was clear in the long-term personnel data for the financial services firm and at the old AT&T. This traditional certainty and stability has been disrupted both by the weakening of traditional silos and by the growing importance of ad hoc teams and projects as strategies for organizing work.

There are some middle managers who enter firms and stay for a long time, moving along predictable paths, but this pattern is no longer the norm. A manager at TechCo described his career as "happenstance," and a look at his internal résumé supports this. He began as a test manager, responsible for running products through their paces. He was then put in charge of TQM programs, and when this position had run its course, he entered a project manager certification program and became responsible for running the firm's project management program. Thinking back on this trajectory, he commented, "I don't mind [moving around], because with each path, I've learned a lot and also bounced all over the company."

While this might seem like a new world of freedom and opportunity, it raises hard questions for these managers. In particular, because the paths ahead are no longer clear, this brings into sharper relief the question of what it takes to succeed, what criteria are being used to judge managers by their superiors. One manager's comment was typical: "I'm puzzled about how to make my next move."

In some cases, the disruptions occur because new organizational forms, teams in particular, create ambiguity. If one's job is to move from one ad hoc project team to another, the strategy for upward mobility becomes unclear. Sometimes, disruptions are due to simple efforts to save money. One manager with whom I talked described what might be termed a classic, old-style career: "Coming out of college, obviously, I was pretty directionless, so I started out just figuring out how could I make some money and not be a beach bum, and my primary interest was in playing basketball at that time. So, I ended up working as a teller and then just went up to the management level within four years, and here I am."

This kind of ascension would no longer be possible, because the pathway from teller to management jobs has been broken. The bank deliberately broke the link by hiring an increasing number of part-time tellers. It is very difficult now to move up from that position.[13]

Career paths have also been disrupted because organizations are flatter. The ladders to the next levels are broken. Since upward mobility requires a spot to move up to, the elimination of these rungs is more than a little disruptive. The evidence is that firms are becoming much flatter. Economists Raghuram Rajan and Julie Wulf find that the number of managers reporting to the CEO in the three hundred largest American firms has increased substantially in recent years, from an average of 4.4 in 1986 to 7.2 in 1999.[14] This implies a substantial flattening in the hierarchy of organizations and the reduction of managerial levels.

A manager at TechCo testified directly to the impact of the changing shape of the corporate pyramid: "I got on the management path really quite early . . . I would say that right now I am puzzled on how to make my next move. What's different is the company is shrinking. So there's not the natural sucking-up to the top."

New business models can also lead to disrupted career paths. For example, at the Bank of America, instead of recruiting managers from the ranks of incumbent employees, the bank now seeks to bring in customer-savvy outsiders from large chains like Wal-Mart. This has made it harder for customer-facing managers to move up, in part because they lack the experience and skills the bank seeks and in part because vacant spots are being filled with outsiders.

CONCLUSION

Restructuring has changed both the opportunities that are available to middle managers and the underlying processes that determine who gets to take advantage of these opportunities. The pathways in firms before restructuring were relatively stable and clear, and while there was more movement into and out of the enterprise than might be implied from extreme versions of the Organization Man, long-term employment and steady ladder-climbing was a reasonable expectation. Although the more traditional pathways have not disappeared entirely, most of today's pathways are more confusing, riskier, and harder to navigate. The long-standing challenges confronting women managers have been exacerbated by restructuring because the increased pressure on hours due to reduced staffing makes work and family concerns even more salient. For everyone, there are fewer steps on the ladder, the spread of teams has made assessment more difficult and has disrupted traditional pathways, and the constant shifting of personnel due to reorganizations has rendered supervision and feedback more problematic. In addition, quite a few middle managers have, for one reason or another, opted out of the advancement game. The assumption that everyone wants to move up the greasy pole is no longer accurate, if it ever was.

If advancement is more problematic, if job security is reduced, and if work is more controlled (as I showed in chapter 4), then there are grounds for worrying about the commitment and loyalty of managers to their employers. But as I also asserted, all the news is not bad. Work may be more controlled, but it is also broader and more interesting and managers retain a strong craft attachment to their tasks. How, then, does this all add up with respect to managerial attitudes toward their employers and toward the larger economic system, of which the managers are part? These are the questions taken up in chapter 6.

Shifting Commitments

Where Do Loyalties Now Lie?

"**M**ark," a manager in his mid-forties, joined Bank of Boston when he graduated from college in the mid-1980s, and he never left. He is an evangelical Christian who travels to missions several times a year. Throughout his office are pictures of him in faraway places standing with groups of children of all colors. While in Boston, he also works on a Christian prison project.

At the time of our first conversation, Mark's career was classic "old school." He had spent a lifetime in the same organization and had prospered as it underwent the transformations associated with mergers. Mark was enthusiastic about his work, he spoke of the "thrill of the role" and managing: "I enjoy coaching and developing employees and, you know, helping them guide their own growth." At the same time, with the merger with Fleet Bank looming, he was seeing changes that boded ill. What bothered him was not simply the fear of losing his lifetime job, but also the gradual change in the atmosphere of the bank. For Mark, what symbolized this was that the bank had stopped holding banquets to celebrate long-term employment anniversaries: "The ceremony is gone, the gift, anything related to recognition. You do not even get a letter when it is your twentieth anniversary." Mark saw a clear message in this: "My read is that it is more what are you doing for me today, not how long have you been doing it."

This disquiet notwithstanding, Mark was committed to his work and to his team. *Enthusiastic* and *upbeat* would be the two adjectives that came most quickly to mind. This positive attitude prevailed despite his not knowing, at the time of our first conversation, if he would have a place with Bank of America after the merger. He had reason to worry; he had heard that the new organization would be flatter and that the team leader position would not be replicated. The rumor turned out to be true. Our next meeting was in a hotel and took place immediately after a coaching session with an outplacement agency. Mark reported that the bank had offered him a position as an independent contributor, but that he had decided that the loss of his managerial position made it difficult for him to stay.

Mark's enthusiasm showed through in the conversation, but not surprisingly, there was an edge. On the one hand, he reported that "I don't have any resentment . . . I actually had choices, which I think allows you not to be bitter." On the other

hand, he spoke bitingly of the dishonesty of the press announce-
ments, in which "Chad Gifford on the Bank of Boston side and
Terry Murray on the Fleet side, especially Chad, kept saying right
in front of cameras that this was a merger of equals. Baloney."
What had also changed for Mark was that he thought his next
job might last only three to five years. His expectations had
adjusted to the new reality.

Six months later, Mark was back at a bank, which was a local
competitor to Bank of America. Despite his refusal of an individual contributor position at his old employer, this was just
what his role was in his new institution. His salary was the same
as before, but for now, he had no bonus. Mark's enthusiasm was
unabated, and he spoke of the pleasure he got from working
with clients and with his colleagues. A victim of the bank
merger, Mark had landed on his feet, albeit in somewhat diminished circumstances. If he felt badly about this, he hid it well.
When it came to his attitudes, Mark seemed somewhat caught
between the old and new worlds. He was clear that any expectations about mutual commitment between employer and
employee were unrealistic and that he and everyone else needed
to think in terms of short-term jobs. At the same time, he obviously hoped and even expected that his new position would last
a long time. Nor did he draw any political conclusions or broad
lessons about corporate behavior. He remained angry at the
senior leadership of Fleet, but when it came to the organization,
he made it clear that "banks are not the public library." They
owed no one anything, in his view, and it was understandable
that they were in the business of maximizing profits for their
shareholders.

In one important respect, Mark's story is not typical of the experience of middle managers. He lost his job, whereas most managers do not. But while most managers are able to hold on to their employment, they certainly live in the same newly insecure world that Mark lives in. The attitudes that Mark displayed represent what might be seen as the mainstream responses of middle managers to their circumstances. Mark is committed to his work, that is, to specific sets of tasks that constitute his job. He enjoys these and finds them fulfilling and is in no sense alienated or rootless. His loyalties are to his workgroup and much less so to his firm. Despite a certain degree of cynicism about the behavior of senior managers, he draws no broader political conclusions about the changing nature of the employment relationship.

MIDDLE MANAGERS ARE CRAFT WORKERS

Middle managers may be under increased pressure and may feel greater stress, but to stop there would miss what is the most important part of the picture. The evidence of the interviews shows a striking pattern: middle managers have strong commitment to the work itself. One TechCo manager, in responding to a question about his job, said that he cared about "building things and getting products out to the customer," and a Bank of America manager responsible for supervising a team who worked with wealthy clients described his job in the same terms, although the product was abstract and not tangible: "One of the thrills . . . is creating portfolios." Another manager at TechCo commented, "I think my job is a nice mix of technical and business. I think

I have a lot of autonomy . . . I get to manage some great guys; they're a lot of fun. Everyone is very motivated. I don't have a morale problem. And it's very dynamic; it's always changing. Six weeks ago, I was managing a technical group, and now I'm off in Asia hiring people. It's very interesting; it's very dynamic. That's what I like about the job."

Comments like these suffused the interviews. Other managers went even further. For example, several of the managers at TechCo were members of an after-hours book club in which they read business books that they felt were relevant to what they were doing at work. A manager at Bank of America was working to build a national association of managers in his particular specialty. The managers with whom I spoke would vigorously disagree with C. Wright Mills' assessment that "the salaried employee does not make anything . . . no product of craftsmanship can be his to contemplate with pleasure."[1]

The best way to think about how these managers value their work is to conceive of them as *craft workers*, a term that is traditionally applied to skilled blue-collar work. The sociologist Randy Hodson identifies four characteristics of craft work: that the work is intrinsically interesting, that employees have an opportunity to use existing skills and learn new ones, that the work is an end as well as a means, and that for employees, the work is an important component of personal identity.[2] There are other ways of thinking about what it means to be a craft worker. An important trait is that the tasks change from day to day and constantly pose new problems. This is in contrast to, say, an assembly line worker, who simply executes the same task every day. Because the tasks and the challenges change, craft

workers need to have an abstract understanding of the principles of their work so that they can successfully adapt to whatever challenge confronts them. Another idea is what might
be termed *craft pride*, that is, a conscious commitment to the
work and to its quality and a set of standards that distinguish
craft work from other, less complex and less quality-conscious
occupations.

Although the term *craft worker* has traditionally been applied
to high-level manual work, it seems an appropriate way to characterize the attitudes of most middle managers. Far from the
cynicism of Robert Jackell ("many lower echelon managers see
themselves as little more than highly paid clerks") and equally
far from the despair of Sennett, the managers whom I interviewed enjoyed their work and took pride in it.[3] Regardless of
how they felt about the changes in the larger environment, most
middle managers are committed to their work and enjoy it.

The craft-worker attitudes of middle managers reinforce the
long-standing point that money is not the most important moti-
vator for most people. Chester Barnard made this argument in
1938 in his class exposition of management theory, which has
been taken up repeatedly since then.[4] It is also important to
understand that these craft workers are not the "professional" or
"organization-hopping" new-style managers highlighted in
some of the more enthusiastic descriptions of the new management world. They remain tied to their organization; it just
happens that they like what they do and are motivated to do a
good job.

One might wonder whether this craft attitude is simply an
adaptive response to diminished opportunities. Perhaps people

who are going nowhere, or whose jobs have been diminished in other ways, compensate by "liking" their work. Even if this observation is accurate, this response is a better adaptation than the responses identified by Rosabeth Kanter for workers who had plateaued in their careers. She emphasized traits such as an overemphasis on peer culture or simple disengagement from the firm. But, in fact, I find no evidence that it is only "unsuccessful" middle managers who have exhibited a craft view of their work. The people who appear to be on the way up, the Nancys of Bank of America or the members of the book club in TechCo, are also committed to what they do. Simply put, while they may have many complaints about their firm and about how the situation in which they find themselves has deteriorated, when it comes to their day-to-day jobs, most middle managers are committed to their work.

WHAT DO MANAGERS THINK ABOUT THEIR EMPLOYERS?

When he characterized managers in the post–World War II period, William H. Whyte wrote that "between themselves and the organization they see an ultimate harmony."[5] He went on to add that the shared assumption was "Be loyal to the company and the company will be loyal to you."[6] The deeper meaning of the Organization Man was that firms were applying the lessons of the Human Relations School of Management, what Daniel Bell critiqued as "cow sociology," to managers as well as to the workers, who were the original target of this line of thinking. The idea was that people yearned for a sense of connection and emotional attachment and that if the firm could provide it, then employees would worry less about potentially conflictual, and distributional, issues such as whether they were paid fairly relative to profits.

Whyte's managers were loyal to their firms and identified with their bosses. The managers respected what the organization did, they expected to be cared for by their firm, and they entertained no subversive thoughts about the ultimate purposes of the corporation or about whether the system in which they were embedded was equitable and fair. This picture can, of course, be exaggerated: in his study of young AT&T managers, Douglas Bray and his colleagues found that over time, the managers' utopian attitudes toward the firm diminished and a realism set in. This simply meant, however, that their attitudes became somewhat less positive, but never turned negative.[7] Half a century later, the objective circumstances of managers are quite different. Although on average many can still expect to keep their jobs, middle managers feel at risk as never before and have witnessed their colleagues being laid off. At the same time, in many organizations, top management is often made up of outsiders who were hired in and who seem to be enriching themselves while simultaneously laying off others below them in the hierarchy. Indeed, in her study of middle managers at Bank of America in the mid-1980s, Vicki Smith found evidence of emerging tensions between top and middle management.[8]

All this raises the obvious question, What are the attitudes of today's middle managers toward their firms and the role of the corporation? Are managers still loyal and committed? Are they politicized and critical? Today's managers may be committed to their jobs in a craft sense, but they are well aware that the nature of their relationship with their employer has shifted. If they were told that the aggregate data suggest that the diminution of security was modest, they would reply that it feels more dramatic on the ground. The new circumstances are an invitation for managers to ask big questions about whether their companies are behaving ethically, about the ultimate purpose of the corporation and its responsibilities to its employees (and to others), and about what political implications might be drawn from what has happened.

To explore these issues, I will ask two broad sets of questions. First, I will examine loyalty. What degree of commitment do the managers feel toward their firms, and what explains the apparent decline in that commitment? Second, I will ask about any broader political or economic conclusions the managers might draw from their circumstances. Do they believe that modern corporate behavior is legitimate, or has their faith in capitalism been shaken?

Loyalty

When Americans are asked about loyalty to their employer, they express considerable ambivalence. The Gallup Poll periodically asks, "Do you have a strong sense of loyalty to the company or organization that you work for, or not?" In 1993, 86 percent expressed strong loyalty, and in 2004, the figure held strong at 85 percent. So, at first glance, all is well. But when asked, "Compared to 20–30 years ago, do you think the average working person in this country shows more loyalty to their employer, less loyalty, or the same?" the responses were 8 percent "more," 51 percent "less," and 37 percent "the same."[9] The obvious implication is that when people respond about themselves, they are giving what is seen as the socially accepted response, but their real sense of things is otherwise.

Among the managers I interviewed, the headline is quite clear: they felt little loyalty to their firm and a very tenuous identification with those at the top. A Bank of America survivor observed, "The degree to which I feel that senior management is . . . I won't say trusted, but respected . . . is variable." A TechCo manager observed that loyalty "has taken a big hit." What is striking is that even successful managers who have learned how to prosper in their organizations are explicit in their lack of commitment. One manager who had not simply survived the Bank of America merger but had also come out in a better position (and who had prepared for our conversation by producing a sheaf of PowerPoint slides describing her job) nonetheless commented:

> I think it has changed a lot in eighteen years. I mean, you
> look at it, so you have a lot more stats in terms of loyalty,
> even in Japan, where everyone is loyal, with the same
> company till the day they die. That will not happen
> anymore . . . I have been here for eighteen years, and I
> wonder if I am stupid or I am just comfortable. And I am
> pretty conservative . . . I cannot say I am loyal . . . I might
> have been able to say that [I was loyal], like, about six
> years or maybe eight or ten years ago, to Bank of Boston.

No manager expressed unalloyed loyalty to his or her employer, and all the managers indicated that their commitment to their firm was tentative and conditional. These were not Organization Men and Women.

As the comments above suggest, there are several distinctive motivations behind the emotional distance the middle managers feel vis-à-vis their employer. For some, the key issue is economic. They feel that their jobs are at risk and that, as a result, they themselves should be more oriented toward the external labor market than their colleagues were in the past. Others are estranged from top management for a variety of reasons that I explore later. In general, there is little outright hostility or anger toward the firm; rather, there is a sense of distance and a lack of the kind of enthusiasm and commitment that one might expect from a management team. These managers are standing back and looking at their firms with a sense of skepticism and caution. This attitude holds for the winners as well as the losers among the middle managers. Virtually no one is "of the corporation."

The most straightforward explanation of the loosened attachment of middle managers to their firms is that their jobs are at risk and that this simple fact leads people to withdraw psychologically if not physically. We have already seen that as a matter of reality, most middle managers will be able to hold on to their jobs, but as a matter of perception and mind-set, their world is much more dangerous than in the past and they react accordingly. The most straightforward expression of this view was by a manager who observed, "I have to protect myself against TechCo." The use of the word "against" is telling. This particular manager thought that TechCo was following the proper path in restructuring and downsizing. Nonetheless, a big gap had opened up between the employee and the employer.

Endemic insecurity directly diminishes loyalty, but can also erode commitment via channels more indirect. One such effect is that as organizations restructure, power struggles and debates about resource allocation break out and can be debilitating:

> You just start sensing some functional bitterness because job security is at stake in that there were whole sections of the organization that other sections would question whether you should just kill that off. "Why should we lose anybody in software engineering when you've got this whole group of people that leave at four o'clock and nobody understands what they do?" That sort of thing . . . It's created some dysfunctionality. People that should be working together being more efficient as a group because they're working together aren't, so you see mistrust and you see two people failing in their individual areas, when if they got together and worked together, they'd both be successful.

Straight Dealing and Greed?

Asked about top management, one person I spoke with commented, "Well, I can tell you that, sort of, there's a very tenuous bond between the leaders and the led. It's sort of a trust issue." The word "trust" is important here because it implies a problem that goes beyond the insecurity that results from market forces beyond anyone's control. Among many of the middle managers, there is a perception that top management is greedy and self-dealing.

These kinds of complaints have come to be echoed throughout public discussions of American business. It is not hard to see why. Several years ago, I invited a senior executive at one of the top executive compensation consulting firms to speak to my class. He worked with the compensation committee of boards of directors to set the pay for the people at the top of the organizations. We discussed pay for performance, and the consultant said, unambiguously, that the very idea was a joke. He said that his role was to identify performance goals that the executives could reach. If the environment changed and these goals became unattainable, he would then come up with a different set of goals. In other words, his objective was to ensure that top management was paid a certain amount, and goal setting was simply a charade to provide a fig leaf of legitimacy to the outcome. He was as clear as he could be in making this point.

Particularly egregious examples often get the most press, as when Hank McKinnell, the former chief executive of Pfizer, received an \$82 million pension and \$200 million in deferred compensation and other benefits, despite the dismal performance of his firm's stock.[10] But the issue goes beyond specific cases. According to one estimate, since the 1980s, the compensation of CEOs at the largest U.S. firms increased by 600 percent and, as a multiple of the average worker's pay, quadrupled to 170 to 1.[11] There are other, somewhat different estimates of the rate of CEO pay growth and the extent of the growing gap between CEOs and everyone else, but all estimates tell the same basic story.[12] The issue has become so controversial that even President George W. Bush weighed in, supporting restraint in a speech at the New York Stock Exchange.[13]

The complaints of the middle managers regarding the pay of those at the top is entirely consistent with the attitudes of most Americans. A 1999 study drew on responses in both America and a broad sample of other developed countries regarding public attitudes toward earnings inequality.[14] In response to the general statement "Income differences are too large," 66 percent of Americans either agreed or strongly agreed. More interesting, however, were the responses to a question about the appropriate pay ratio of the highest-paid occupation to average pay. In the survey, the highest-paid occupation was defined as chief executive officer. American attitudes were nearly identical to those of other nations: the ethically acceptable ratio was thought to be 3 to 1. Given that the actual ratio in the United States is about 170 to 1, it is clear that the average American views CEO pay as well out of line.

For example, CEO Chad Gifford obtained a sweet deal after selling Fleet to Bank of America: a $24.3 million severance bonus; $3.1 million in retirement income per year for life; a private jet that he can use for any purpose, including personal; and four tickets to fifteen Red Sox games per year for life.[15] It is not hard to think that Fleet managers who faced layoffs would have some strong feelings about this over-the-top reward for Gifford. And their colleagues who managed to hold on to their jobs were probably also unhappy. Nancy, the lending manager who, as described in chapter 1, survived the layoffs despite her travails and who is generally sympathetic to the need to restructure ("prune" for organizational health is the way she puts it) was nonetheless unhappy with executive greed: "It ticks me off . . . What ticks me off is that [we should be asking] where's the decision in all that? . . . It seems a bad example, because there are other people who I think have made a lot of money who really didn't deserve it." Her take on this is widely shared.

It was not just Fleet managers who felt that the top layers were greedy and self-interested. Many managers at TechCo also believed that top management feathered its own nest at the expense of the rest of the firm, and the complaints had two components. The first was that when the large-scale layoffs were executed, the folks at the top protected themselves. As one manager put it, "One of the things that I think was a problem at the time was that there was a perception that managers were not touchable when the layoffs came around. It was more that all the people at the bottom were getting cut out and none of the senior men was getting laid off." Second, TechCo managers shared the same worries as their brethren at Fleet regarding imbalanced compensation structures.

Broken Ladders' Effect on Loyalty

Top-management greed is corrosive, but, in some important sense, is not structural. In many firms, doubtlessly the majority, those at the top are certainly sensitive to these issues and believe in shared pain and some measure of equity. A structural shift in the circumstances of middle managers, however, also leads them to feel more distant from their leaders. This is the disruption of career paths and the increased difficulty in making a move from the middle to the top. Middle managers today have less reason to believe that they are on a trajectory to move to the top and therefore have less reason to identify with their bosses.

In Japan, senior executives are groomed from the lower ranks and their development is closely managed by a powerful human resource department that moves people around the organization to develop their skills. Some American firms operated very similarly with respect to managers, and indeed, the best-practice firms such as IBM and General Electric were famous for their management development programs. Although not the same in the details, many American firms resembled Japan's with their closed, internal labor markets and upward-mobility paths for managers. Another version is the more political story told by Jackell. In his view, new top managers, on their promotion, reached into the ranks and pulled up their acolytes with them.[16] In either case, the main line is clear: middle managers were part of a conveyer belt leading to the top, and they had ample reason to identify with their superiors.

For middle managers today, the path upward is much more problematic. I have already described one source of this difficulty, the delayering of the firm. As described earlier, there is substantial flattening in the hierarchy of organizations and a reduction of managerial levels.[17] However, the nature of the shift is deeper than this. Two illustrations of the pattern come from Bank of America. At the bottom of the ladder, the teller jobs used to be staging points for a modest managerial career, but these jobs have been increasingly made part-time and lower-skilled, with many of their tasks shifted to managers who are expected to work the floor.[18] More importantly, the company is increasingly inclined to hire managers from the outside rather than promote from within. For example, the bank wants to instill greater consumer awareness in its system and therefore has recruited branch managers from large retail chains such as Wal-Mart. In other parts of the bank, the organization has also shown an increased willingness to bring in talent from the outside.

The most dramatic example of the opening up of the internal ladder to the outside is the increased willingness of firms to hire their CEO from outside rather than promote from within. Using the *Forbes* Magazine database on CEOs (covering over thirteen hundred firms), Michael Jensen and Kevin Murphy calculate that in the 1970s, 14.9 percent of new CEOs were outside hires; in the 1980s, it was 17.2 percent; and in the 1990s, the percentage shot up even more, to 26.5 percent.[19] This pattern demonstrates the increased disruption of standard career paths. An additional sign of the growing distance of the top from the rest of the organization is data that show that the compensation gap between the CEO and the rest of the top executive team was stable for most of the postwar period, but started rising in the early 1990s and had more than doubled by 2006.[20]

The impact of bringing in an outsider is amplified by two related considerations. First, the outsider is likely to take an adversarial stance vis-à-vis the organization since implicitly his or her hiring was the result of alleged failures in that organization. As a result, the career advancement of many internal managers is disrupted. This will be amplified by the loss of "pull" from an incumbent CEO.

Second, middle managers used to feel cut from the same cloth as the leaders of their organization. In some sense, the managers felt class solidarity. The sources of this identification are easy to identify. Because top management was typically drawn from the lower ranks in the organization, people felt a sense of familiarity and identification as well as the expectation that advancement was well within the possibilities for middle management. The recently broken ladders have altered all this, and middle managers need to search for new loyalties.

To What Are They Loyal?

Managers have a tenuous loyalty to their employer. They are loyal to their work in that they are very much like craft workers. But if they are not loyal to the firm or to top management, where, if anywhere, do their affective commitments lie? As it turns out, these managers do have fairly intense commitments, one of which is concrete and another of which looks perhaps to an idealized view of the past.

The concrete commitments is hardly surprising: managers are very loyal to their immediate colleagues and their work group. "I love my staff," and "My real loyalties are to the work group" are typical comments. These sentiments are unsurprising and are only notable in the context of the absence of loyalty to the broader institution. But when combined with the craft commitment to the work itself, the strong commitment that managers have to their work group implies that the turmoil in managerial ranks may have a fairly minimal impact on work effort. After all, managers who both enjoy their tasks and care about their colleagues are likely to keep on trying to do the best they can, even in the face of real tensions with the rest of the organization and those who are leading it. And consistent with this, the interviews produced very little evidence that the managers were withholding effort.

The more unexpected pattern was that in both Bank of America and TechCo, the managers are also loyal to their image of the past. In both organizations, many managers have constructed a perhaps idealized portrait of what their employers used to be like. What's more, the managers maintain quite strong commitments to this vision. This is not quite the same as expecting to return to the old days of stable employment and corporate loyalty, an expectation that Charles Heckscher found when he interviewed managers in the early 1990s.[21] That hope is no longer reasonable, and no one holds to it. But the pull of the past does remain strong.

At Bank of America, the managers look back to either the culture of Bank of Boston, the last of the big banks swallowed by Fleet prior to the Bank of America merger, or else to Fleet itself. Virtually all the managers agree that the Fleet and Bank of Boston cultures were very different, and depending on where they worked, they speak nostalgically of the old days. "Many people still identify themselves with the legacy bank" is how one manager put it. Bank of Boston people describe their old organization as softer and more caring, with less emphasis on hard-edged performance measures. The implication is that the layoffs that occurred under both Fleet and Bank of America would not have happened under Bank of Boston. As one manager put it, "Bank of Boston was more ready to compensate you for doing a good job, and number two, they were more willing to promote. There seems to be in my opinion, a lot less . . . politics, a lot less jockeying. " By contrast, the Fleet partisans pointed to what they saw as a greater emphasis on performance and higher expectations. Both sides reported that they tended to socialize with people from their side of the divide.

At TechCo, the old days are symbolized by the firm's founder, who continued to run the company until about five years before my interviews. In part, managers felt that the organizational style changed with the transition to the new leadership: "The organization has changed. You can put your finger on it. You know, you can back up the clock from the last CEO . . . put your finger right on it. Much more of an operational flair. Everything was in process. Everything had to be predictable. Everything had to be measurable, and I just think that . . . everything isn't. I don't know who was quoted as saying this, but managers lead people and manage process. I think we've just, to some extent, been just beaten to snot." In addition, the general view was that under the old regime, top management was more willing to share the sacrifices entailed by the cyclical nature of the industry. This was sometimes blamed on outsiders who were hired by the new top managers: "I see [one upper manager] come in; he has come in from the outside . . . I think he's had an influence on the rest of them in terms of, 'Hey, we're worth more than we're getting paid.' I kind of think that . . . has had that influence on the rest of the group."

It is hard to judge the accuracy of these depictions of the past. Although they are certainly widely shared within each organization, this does not make them accurate. In large measure, however, the accuracy of the views is beside the point. The managers have lost their capacity to have a strong affective commitment to the organization as it is perceived today and have turned to the past to fill this gap. Over time, this will most likely fade, both because the past will become more distant and less compelling and because the populations in the organizations will gradually include larger numbers of new employees, for whom this particular past is irrelevant. The important point is the circumscribed nature of managerial loyalty, which is given to the small work group and to the past, not to the larger organizations where managers labor today.

THINKING MORE BROADLY

Managers are not loyal to their organization; they feel distant from those at the top, and what loyalties they have are to small work groups and a perhaps idealized image of the past. How does all this translate into the managers' perceptions about the purposes of the firm and the legitimacy of the system in which they live? The hopeful social critics who believed that white-collar employees might someday constitute a new class that would ally with the traditional working class against the bosses could hardly have hoped for a better scenario than the waves of layoffs that have swept through corporations. Surely, the sight of senior management firing thousands of people while increasing their own salaries and perks would set off some kind of serious reaction. Even setting aside the more fevered speculations, it is certainly reasonable to ask how the years of restructuring have affected the political views of middle managers. Do they believe that the layoffs are expressions of legitimate goals of the corporation, or have managers become critics of the operation of American-style capitalism?

The standard view of these questions, the perspective that was the first instinct of most of managers with whom I talked, was expressed by "Rodney." In his late fifties, Rodney oversaw a group of accountants at Fleet. He had several sources of anger toward his employer, most particularly a fear that he would lose his job because of his age. He saw this as possible age discrimination.

He was also upset with some of the severance packages that top Fleet managers received as they exited the firm. Nonetheless, his views about what the corporation owes its employees were conventional: "That's business in America, [so you'd] better deal with it. You know, what are you going to do about it? I put my best foot forward and hope for the best [and] meanwhile look elsewhere. I don't think companies owe their employees anything. You know, if you're fortunate enough to have a job, you just do everything you can to keep it." The starkest presentation of this perspective was put forward by a manager at TechCo: "It's a business . . . The company has to make money . . . the people owe X amount of work for their paycheck."

This view, that the relationship between the employee and the firm is purely transactional, is an argument used by many managers I interviewed. Another version is that restructuring is necessary to maintain the economic health of the firm and hence is in fact an action for the greater good. The views of this manager were typical:

> I tend to look at it from a very objective kind of rational
> perspective, I think, which is [TechCo] as an entity has
> to be profitable or the company goes out of business, in
> which case all six thousand employees lose their job. And
> so if we have to lay off a couple hundred employees in
> order for the company to be viable, it's unfortunate—
> obviously nobody likes to do that, but it's one of those
> things that kind of comes with playing in this game.
> So from that perspective, I understand why it happens.
> I understand that it's a necessity.

At one level, it is not surprising that the managers expressed these views. Several international comparative studies of the political and social views of managers have found that, in the words of one review, "American managers are outliers . . . [with] their extreme individualism and market orientation."[22] The standard explanation lies in the weak role that government played in early industrialization and hence the sense of self-reliance that managers developed as well as the lack of a strong union movement or other social forces that could force management to cooperate with a larger society. The consequence was that individualism has long been the dominant American managerial perspective.

The problem with the arguments many of the managers made is that there is a series of subtleties that sometimes gets lost. If the firm has no more commitment to its employees than it would to any stranger, then why should the firm expect the employees to make any greater effort or care more about its success than would a stranger? If the relationship is purely financial and short term, then this would seem to set limits to what the employees will do. This point was made very clearly by a TechCo manager when he reflected on his experience at his former employer, General Electric, and the attitude of then CEO Jack Welch toward the employees:

> This was in the eighties, eighty-five. I'd be working there at ten o'clock at night, and I'd go in Saturday morning, if something broke down, and fix it. I was into it. I remember this one time, Welch made this statement that at the end of every week—Friday evening—we're even. I was

like, "Fuck you, I'm here Saturday." You need to acknowl-
edge that there's more than just . . . It's not that simple,
because there's a value to emotional bond. When people
put that extra in, there's extra value that you squeeze out.
And somehow, that has to get acknowledged.

Even beyond this is an issue about to whom the corporation
is responsible. Is it responsible just to the shareholders or some
combination of shareholders, employees, and perhaps other
constituencies? Ultimately, after these issues are thought
through, the transactional perspective may still make the most
sense, but the issues deserve careful consideration.

I explored these questions with "Tom," a seasoned middle
manager at TechCo. Tom has been at TechCo for over twenty
years, all on the operations side. He was not one of the rocket
scientists who designed, or managed the design of, the new
products. Rather, he was an engineering manager responsible
for building the product and getting it out the door. Because of
his seniority and obvious intelligence, he was fairly high up the
managerial food chain.

In discussing with Tom how he assessed the fairness and
appropriateness of layoffs, I found myself violating political cor-
rectness (which forbids sports analogies) and drawing parallels
with Bill Belichick, the coach of the very successful New England
Patriots football team. The National Football League operates
with a salary cap, which means that a team has a limit on its
payroll. Like the budget constraint facing a firm, the cap means
that a dollar spent on one player is a dollar less that you can
spend on another. In this regime, Belichick is famous for his

totally unsentimental attitude toward his players. If a player appears expensive relative to his performance, if the dollars can get more value with another player, then Belichick has no compunction about firing that player. This holds, regardless of how long the player has been with the team or how much he has contributed in the past. There is no loyalty, only a pure cost-to-benefit calculus.

I asked Tom how he thought about this in the context of TechCo. Was this the right way to run a corporation? This conversation is worth quoting at some length because it captures many of the key themes.

Facilitator: Belichick seems to have the view that you're his friend until you're not. So using that analogy, there are two views of companies. One view is that what I owe you is this week's pay. What you owe me is this week's work, and we'll see about next week when next week comes. Another view is kind of a community, there's kind of a mutual commitment. How do you think about that?

Interviewee: Yeah, I absolutely understand it. And I'll take the two sides. This is one of those interesting questions. From a Patriots fan, if so-and-so wasn't going to help the team win or was going to be overpriced and cost us a linebacker and a safety, hey . . . get out of there, baby . . . Now, I'm in the locker room and one of these guys: you look and you say, what's in it for me to show loyalty to take the pay cut to do that? And the answer is, there isn't a lot. So I understand that.

Now my view of [TechCo] is we've had a management team, middle management and others, and they're kind of at the end of their careers, and for the most part, they have stayed on, and some have been pushed aside and into other jobs, while the new guys have been brought up. But very rarely has [TechCo] released the guys ... These guys did great work for a number of years and were no longer effective, and it takes years to have them finally leave or whatever. So I think TechCo is not taking the Belichick mode of "Hey, I owe you this paycheck, that's it, have a nice life!" I think they're more in the "Let's keep on, even if the ankle's gone and their knee's gone, they're hobbling, but they can play a role off the bench."

Facilitator: So how do you feel about it?

Interviewee: Whether it's sports or TechCo, I look certainly from the viewpoint of, if people don't think I'm pulling my own weight, tell me and I'll be out of here tomorrow.

Facilitator: So you're Bill Belichick?

Interviewee: From a personal viewpoint, yes. For me. Now, have I had at least one or two of these guys that had been here for a long time? I've had more than that. I've laid off two of them over the years—nice guys, actually, two of the guys that I laid off. One was my first office mate, and one was the guy who initially trained me. And those are tough decisions to make and tough calls, but again, what am I gonna bet on? And for the other X thousands of people in the company and the stockholders and for my own future, for that matter ... I don't think Belichick did anything wrong.

Facilitator: How about in terms of larger-scale layoffs, not individuals but kind of hundreds of people in outgoings and downturns? Does the company have an obligation to try and soften those, or is it responsible only to the stockholder?

Interviewee: I think we have to be more careful in some of those. The last downturn was tough because of the length, the time, but the continuing [for those who kept their jobs], you know . . . You talked about morale. When [you have lay-offs for] three quarters in a row or whatever it was, . . . it's impossible to have meaningful conversations with people about the future, because things become so uncertain. So you're into the interesting conversation of what's better for these—like capitalism. The downside of capitalism is it's short term. So, when you go through some of these things, the reality of today is pretty harsh and you make decisions and you hurt yourself in the long term because you need to satisfy today's shareholder demands.

Keeping good people [is hard], and the company pushes a lot on, "Who are your key contributors? Make sure they know they're not at risk." On the other hand, those people have friends who have been affected, and that takes away their loyalty. To me, it's the environment. If you're a good person and you know you can go get a job in a whole bunch of different places, geez, do I want to work with a guy and then see him screwed over by the company? Probably not. So, you're more at risk for those things. So I think there's some reasonable risk-taking you have to take in any of these jobs.

Facilitator: Can the company do that? Can the company tell the shareholders, "Listen, you're gonna get a lower return today because there's long-term benefits here in doing that"?

Interviewee: Only if you deliver.

Tom, bright and thoughtful as he is, is obviously of two minds. On the one hand, both for himself and for the firm, he sees a need to be fairly ruthless and "business-minded." On the other hand, he also believes that too tough a line is bad for morale and hurts the performance of survivors. And leaving costs and benefits aside, he also thinks it is important to be loyal to people who built the firm, even if they are no longer quite pulling their weight. In short, he sees the situation from multiple angles and in the end is conflicted.

Doing Layoffs Right

Most of the managers in both firms had clear views about the appropriate way to restructure. As a first step, they made a clear distinction between poor individual performance and the impact of the impersonal forces such as the business cycle or mergers. There was a general view that people who did not carry their weight did not deserve whatever protection the firm might be able to afford, but the same people who expressed this fairly standard view also went on to comment that employees who had contributed to the firm over a number of years did in fact deserve some special consideration: "Theoretically, when we're doing these layoffs, we're not laying people [off] for performance. It's different from laying somebody off for performance. 'You can't do the job; that was a mistake, sorry.' Let them go. You don't owe that individual anything. But if somebody's come in here and performed for you and helped you succeed, particularly as a management team, managers can't do jack without people that report to them. I can't get all the things done that I'm responsible for. I need those people."

The distinction between laying off for performance and doing so because of the cycle is not always clear. Some of the professional macroeconomics literature argues that firms systematically use the business cycle as an excuse for restructuring and for pruning their weakest employees. The managers at TechCo were sensitive to this, but it did not alter their views that there are basic standards for doing layoffs "right":

> Well, I think we owe them a lot. I mean, we don't have
> the McDonald's hiring model. We've always described
> ourselves as high-end career employers. So if we're
> letting someone go, particularly in a layoff, we're really
> not being intellectually honest with ourselves. We're not
> laying off for performance. We're laying somebody off
> because we've got to downsize. Then, Jesus, that individ-
> ual has probably worked with us for a number of years.
> I think that we at least owe them a reasonable package.
> We at least owe helping them through the transition . . .
> I also think that we use the layoff systematically to trim
> people from the mob. We're not saying that out loud, but
> to anybody who's paying attention, it's obvious.

Another TechCo manager found himself caught in the middle:

> I don't feel like the organization is at either extreme,
> and I personally don't feel at either extreme. I'm not

somebody who's of the opinion that if you've been with the company for twenty-five years, then you sort of get a free ticket automatically. But I'm also in the camp that you do need to understand the context of people's experience, what they have done for the company over the years, to factor that . . . variety of considerations. To me it's more of a balance, and [I] have a sort of feeling that [it] is the environment here. I don't think when you're talking about either compensation or job security that people believe that there is safety in years of experience, but I don't think people believe it's just a cutthroat "This person is costing us this many dollars, and the return . . . from this person is this many dollars."

The idea of cutting some slack to long-term employees whose performance was no longer adequate might, at first glance, seem like a consequence of sentimentality and therefore inconsistent with the pure transactional view. Such a practice might not seem well aligned with the Bill Belichick School of Management. But if the effort of productive employees depends on their feeling that either they or their colleagues will be taken care of when or if their productivity declines, then a softer policy indeed makes sense, even for Bill Belichick and his followers. In fact, evidence from my interviews suggests that the managers' level of effort depends on how fairly they think their colleagues have been treated.

The Views of Young Managers

The managers at Bank of America and TechCo are loyal to their co-workers and, in an abstract way, loyal to the past. But the managers are not especially committed to their organization; nor do they generally respect those at the top who are leading their organizations. Views vary considerably about whether the firm should be willing to trade off some profits in the interests of stakeholders other than the stock owners. The managers do not, however, draw any broad political conclusions from their situation and they continue to support "the system" as they understand it.

Many of the managers I interviewed were middle-aged and had been with their employer for a substantial number of years. They seem likely to give their firms the benefit of the doubt, and so the fraying of commitment and loyalty is even more striking. But what about younger managers? Are they even more distanced from their employers? To answer this question, I surveyed MBA graduates from the classes of 2000 and 2005 at MIT Sloan. I asked them about their assessment of how their employers make decisions and about their own degree of loyalty and commitment.[23]

What do these young managers think their firms value? To get at this, I asked them to divide one hundred points among four objectives in proportion to what weight they thought their employer gave to each objective when it made important strategic decisions. The results of this exercise are shown in table 6-1.[24]

What is striking about these responses is the low weight given to employees and the relatively high weight given to the self-interest of the decision makers themselves. It is not hard to imagine the consequences when senior management is perceived as giving high value to its own self-interest as it plots the future of the enterprise. The implications are in fact played out when I asked the young managers the standard questions found

TABLE 6-1

How young MBAs view their organization's priorities

Objective	Perceived importance*
Interests of stock owners	28
Interests of employees	19
Interests of customers	31
Interests of top management	25

Source: Data from author's survey of 308 MBA graduates from the classes of 2000 and 2005 at MIT Sloan School of Management.

* Number of points, out of 100, survey respondents believe the company would ascribe to the objective.

in the literature to test commitment: their willingness to work harder than they need to for the firm's success and their degree of loyalty to the firm. Their replies are recorded in table 6-2.

Keeping in mind that these are young elite MBAs, the lack of loyalty and absence of extra effort is quite striking. Barely more

TABLE 6-2

Young MBAs' loyalty to their organization

Willing to work harder than necessary for the firm's success:

Strongly agree	34.5%
Somewhat agree	18.7%

Feel little loyalty to the firm:

Strongly agree	17.5%
Somewhat agree	30.8%

Source: Data from author's survey of 308 MBA graduates from the classes of 2000 and 2005 at MIT Sloan School of Management.

than half were willing to work harder than necessary for the firm's success, and just under a half report that they lack loyalty to the firm. It seems fair to conclude that the continual rounds of restructuring and the prevalence of the view that "we're even on Friday" has had significant consequences.

CONCLUSION

Middle managers are committed to their tasks, to their immediate jobs, and to their close colleagues. In addition, they broadly accept the view that some degree of restructuring and layoffs is necessary, given economic realities. From the firm's perspective, this is all to the good. The bad news is that the middle managers have lost their commitment to the firm as an enterprise and they are deeply suspicious of the motivations and actions of top management. These negative reactions are even more apparent in the young MBA graduates whom I surveyed. This is disturbing because the younger managers do not have the kind of long history and personal attachments that might color the attitudes of their older colleagues whom I interviewed in TechCo and Bank of America.

What to make of these conflicting attitudes is unclear. Should firms feel sanguine because the middle managers have a craftlike commitment to their work? Should employers worry that the lack of loyalty presages a lack of effort? How should we, outside observers, assess the situation? And what, if anything, should be done? These are the questions that I take up in chapter 7.

7

Middle Management

Today and Tomorrow

Maybe one reason why things are so f—d up in the organization these days is guys running off, not listening to middle management.

—Christopher Moltisanti, in "46 Long," episode on *The Sopranos*

Middle managers are here to stay. As their ranks have grown, the extreme predictions of the management bashers have not come to pass. Nonetheless, the circumstances of middle managers have been transformed in significant ways.

Layoffs are the most obvious new circumstance, and while most middle managers hold on to their jobs, insecurity is much more of an issue than in the past. One way to think about this is to imagine a large work group with a stable and long-serving membership. One day, a few people are suddenly fired. Although the statistician might point out that the percentage fired is very low, the reality is that everyone's world has changed. People's expectations are different, and their anxiety is higher.

The changes confronting middle management, however, go well beyond insecurity. The nature of work has shifted as firms engage in process reengineering and make greater use of ad hoc and project teams. Upward mobility is now more problematic because rungs have been removed from the ladder and because constant reorganizations have introduced a new element of uncertainty and randomness into the process.

On the other hand, we also saw that middle managers should not be considered victims. It is hard to interview managers and recognize the stick figures in the literature: the helpless, characterless employees of C. Wright Mills; the loyal slaves of William H. Whyte; the lost souls of Richard Sennett; the vicious political animals of Robert Jackell. None of this captures reality. Most middle managers have craft attitudes toward their work and derive a great deal of satisfaction from what they do.

Even this craft commitment has a double edge. While middle managers are committed to their work, they are also more alienated from their organizations and more removed from top management. They are increasingly less likely to be promoted into those ranks, their compensation has fallen behind that of the top, and they believe that top management has behaved unfairly and feathered its own nests.

Bank of America is in most respects a "traditional" firm, while TechCo is more representative of the "new" economy. But remarkably, the basic story is the same in both enterprises. The only systematic difference between the two settings is the greater use of project and ad hoc teams in TechCo. This difference creates the appearance of more job changing at TechCo. Indeed, people do move more in the sense that their work settings and specific assignments vary. However, they still tend to stay within the same broad functional chimneys, and the overall pattern is the same as that at the bank. Only fleetingly do we glimpse the newly fulfilled "intrapreneurs" of the new pop management literature. Beyond this, however, the experiences of middle managers at the two firms are similar with respect to autonomy, control, promotions, gender, and connection to the larger organization and senior management.

THE SMALL-WORLD PROBLEM

The attitudes of middle managers toward their careers is complex, composed of multiple strands. They take craft pride in the work and feel loyal to their colleagues. Their ambition is, by and large, limited; many managers are willing to make some trade-offs in their careers to improve their family life. But while committed to their tasks and to their colleagues, they have become alienated from top management, and their commitment to their firm is conditional and tentative.

The best way to think about these managers is that they live in a small world and have limited horizons. One manager spoke of living in "my own little world," which captures the general frame of mind. Only two of all the managers I interviewed saw their work as having some higher purpose. One, Mark, from chapter 6, connected his work to his religious commitments, while a manager at TechCo spoke of designing components that saved lives by making air bags more effective. But these were exceptions. The rest of the managers were focused on their day-to-day jobs, were committed to their colleagues, felt distant from their firm, saw no larger purpose in what they were doing, and drew no political conclusions from anything that had happened to them or to the economy.

In chapter 6, I explained that middle managers are nostalgic about the past, but also live in something of a fantasy world about the future. When Ely Chinoy interviewed blue-collar automobile skilled craftsmen in the 1950s, he observed that many of them talked about opening their own business at some point.[1] The managers I spoke with were the same. In the interviews, many managers were happy to talk about what they hoped to do if they could leave the company. Their goals ranged from finding another similar job to teaching motorcycle safety, teaching airplane pilot courses, opening a small business, or going to work for a nonprofit. The point is that well over half of the managers had thought about alternative plans. Whether they actually do these things is another question, but the existence of these plans in the forefront of their minds speaks a good deal about their frame of mind.

The essence of the Organization Man was that he (or she) "belonged" to the corporation and had a broader commitment than just to the job and the immediate work group. Managers have the same "need for attachment" that Elton Mayo and the Human Relations School attributed to workers, but in the past, the firm itself met this need. Because of the combination of the obvious lack of loyalty that firms demonstrate toward their employees and the examples of top management greed, these broader loyalties have dissipated. In this sense, middle managers have become more like ordinary workers and today lack the larger commitment to the organization that might distinguish them from the mass of employees. Nevertheless, middle managers are in no sense a new class. In the 1950s, William Whyte observed that unlike academics and literary people, managers have no politics, an observation that remains true.[2] Middle managers have not developed any larger political critique and remain committed to the overall economic system.

The small world does not mean that managers are bitter or alienated. As I have shown, they like their work and are committed to their colleagues. Middle managers have lost respect for the people at the top and are skeptical that their firms will take care of them. They are, in other words, caught between conflicting attitudes and emotions. All the ramifications of the change in middle management sensibilities may be somewhat unclear, but it is important to try to understand them.

MOVING AHEAD

The small-world perspective of middle managers enables them to survive, and sometimes prosper, in the new environment. This frame of mind, however, is also limiting and disturbing. It means that the managers are neither truly committed to their employers nor fully engaged in executing the firm's strategy. This is a drawback for the firm and a source of frustration for the managers themselves. Peter Drucker recognized the risk of this disengagement long ago, noting that managers' concerns with the technical details of their work might lead them to lose sight of the bigger picture.[3] Adding to the worry is the troubling evidence from my survey of recent MBA graduates. In this survey, I found that they hold what can only be termed a deeply cynical view of their employers.

Moving beyond the small-world perspective requires two major steps. The first is to find ways to enable people to build careers and experience a sense of progress within the organization despite the diminished opportunities for upward mobility. The second strategy is to directly address the widely perceived sense of unfairness and inequity in the behavior of top management.

How can we improve the circumstances of middle managers and help firms take better advantage of their talent? One view is to move entirely to a transactional, pack-your-own-parachute ("on Friday, we're even") perspective. The problem is that this misreads the reality of managerial work and careers. Although job security has declined, most middle managers still spend most of their careers with one employer or, at most, a few. A high rate of job changing is not the norm; nor is it likely to be. Effective managers need to understand their organizations, and this deep tacit knowledge and ability to utilize informal as well as formal channels can only come with substantial tenure.

The implication of this line of thought is that moving ahead requires a set of small and large steps. The "human resource management" practices of firms should change to create careers that are realistic for middle managers, given continued long-term employment and the elimination of rungs in the promotion ladder. At the same time, the larger problem of alienation can only be addressed by rethinking the behavior of top management and the purposes of the firm.

Building Careers

Not all managers want to move up the hierarchy. But virtually all have a strong craft attachment to their work. For those who want to move up, the new environment creates substantial difficulties. And for those who do not, there remains the question of how to enable these people to build their skills and to obtain a broader sense of the purposes of the organization. Better career systems would help overcome some of the problems of the small-world vision.

There are certain obvious blocking-and-tackling steps that can help. Frequent, almost faddish, reorganizations are disruptive in their own right and have subtle impacts such as creating instability in supervision. If people's supervisors are only in place for short periods and are abruptly yanked away, then career planning becomes very hard. In a similar vein, organizations can do a better job than they have in articulating the metrics against which people are judged.

The deeper challenge, however, is how to build careers when there are fewer rungs on the ladder. Other researchers have, not surprisingly, addressed this question. One of the most thoughtful is Charles Heckscher, who studied restructuring in several large firms in the late 1980s and early 1990s. He takes very much a free-agent view of the relationship between managers and their organizations: "The assumption is that the match between individual and organization is a temporary one, defined by the frame of the project or mission. That fact that you've done your best for twenty years is not the point, and entails no obligation on the part of the company; contributing to the current direction of the firm is what matters."[4] Heckscher recognizes that this relationship can have very negative consequences if managers are simply cut loose. His solution is that managers build a "community of purpose" based on an external commitment to their profession. They would come to think of themselves much the way that other independent professions, say, doctors and lawyers, do. That is, managers' primary commitment would be to their profession and the relevant professional organizations (some of which, in the case of managers, would have to be created), and their attachment to any particular employer would be transitory. Supporting public institutions, such as portable health insurance and effective labor market intermediaries to help with job matching, would grease the system and make it work.

This is a powerful vision, but is it realistic? There are increasing commonalities between managers and other professions, but these similarities work in the opposite direction from what the independent vision implies. Doctors and lawyers—the professionals supposedly providing a model for managers—today find themselves increasingly working in large bureaucracies. A better analogy than the classic professions might be the new craft and technical occupations that have grown up around the Internet. Many skilled professionals, such as computer programmers or graphic artists, work as independent contractors, and new institutions have grown up to support them. For example, one such institution—Working Today—has found a way to pool independent contractors so that they can obtain affordable health insurance; the organization also serves as a job-finding network. Other professional associations, such as the Graphic Artists Guild, perform similar functions.

In fact, the image of computer professionals making their own way and creating new institutions as they move from firm to firm may be attractive, even romantic, but it is also an exaggeration. For example, in 2006, among computer and mathematics professionals with at least a college degree, 55 percent had five or more years of tenure with their employer, compared with 63 percent for managers.[5] There is a difference, but not a huge one. Most employees in these categories work within organizations and intend to stay with them. As further evidence, a recent study that tracked the careers of recent computer science graduates with a college degree or higher found that only 5 percent of all the jobs held by the graduates were as independent contractors and less than 10 percent of the sample had any experience as contractors.[6]

More seriously, the difficulty with this image of "free-range" managers is that it poorly fits the realities of managerial work. First, as demonstrated clearly in the job-tenure data in chapter 3, most managers do spend long stretches of time with the same employer, a situation that fits managers' aspirations. Second, the nature of managerial work is such that a great deal of firm-specific knowledge is required to function effectively. A manager who moves from firm to firm as a hired gun cannot understand the culture and norms of the organizations in which he or she works. Nor can the person get a grip on the specific policies, procedures, and politics that make each organization distinctive.

How then should organizations go about building internal careers? In part, the idea is to take advantage of the craft orientation of managers and emphasize the opportunity to hone existing skills and develop new ones. The commitment of managers to their tasks is a major advantage in career building. But craft commitment is not enough, because, as we saw, it is part of the small-world phenomenon. One way of thinking about what has to be done is to raise managers' perceived status from a craft to a profession. Exactly what constitutes a profession has been debated in the literature, but the best formulation is that of Andrew Abbott, who argues that a profession is based on the presence of a set of abstract ideas about the subject matter (as opposed to the traditional definitions that emphasized, for example, an ethics code or a professional organization).[7] In his view, auto mechanics is a craft while medicine is a profession because the former lacks the theoretical body of knowledge that the latter possesses. Abbott focuses on the abstract set of ideas because they enable the profession to survive in competition with other professions, to "redefine its problems and tasks, defend them from interlopers, and seize new problems."[8]

For the purposes of this discussion, the competition among professions for control over tasks is less important than the notion of creating a larger vision that can sustain people inside organizations even if they are not moving up. There has been a great deal of recent discussion regarding the role of the MBA, with many critics arguing that business schools are doing a poor job of preparing managers. Most critics argue that too few practical skills are being taught, a line of thought that overlooks the need to develop a stronger core body of abstract knowledge and professional orientation. Instead, MBA education should provide students with a broad sense of themselves as managerial professionals and not simply marketers or investment bankers or consultants.[9]

Despite the importance of education, most of the heavy lifting to raise the horizons of managers and to overcome the small-world orientation has to be done by firms. Firms need to create career paths that do not entirely rest on upward mobility and that expose their managers to a broader view of the enterprise. One way to accomplish this is to encourage and permit more horizontal movement across positions and to facilitate this movement by increasing internal training opportunities. The IBM plan to create a training account along the lines of an individual retirement account with a company match is a step in this direction. It is a start, even though the requirement that employees make a contribution tilts the plan toward easing departures from the firm as opposed to a plan to encourage more internal mobility.

At the same time that horizontal mobility is increased, managers should be systematically exposed via training and contact with top management to a larger vision of the purposes and strategy of the enterprise. TechCo has taken a small step in this direction by creating a management development program for a small subset of middle managers. This program uses weekly seminars to expose the managers to senior leaders who speak about the challenges and the strategies of the organization and provides some modest skill training. The managers with whom I spoke and who were part of this program were on average less alienated from the firm than the rest of the managerial workforce. Efforts like these should be more broadly available.

There is also a role for public policy. While most managers will not lose their jobs, these businesspeople are clearly more at risk than in the past. We saw, for example, that dislocation rates have risen. More training investments by their employers is a step toward helping these people find new work, but public policy investments are also important. People who study dislocation agree that two central steps are important. The first is to decouple health insurance from employers so that the risks of dislocation are reduced. Second, although we had formerly not invested in labor market intermediaries that could help skilled employees find new jobs, because the need was minimal, such institutions are now important in the newly fluid and dangerous job market and should be developed.[10]

FAIRNESS

Middle managers are broadly committed to their job as it is narrowly defined. Their commitment to their employer, on the other hand, is very tenuous. Part of the explanation lies in the new uncertainties that they face in their careers, but an additional, important factor is the widely held view that top management has behaved unfairly, feathering its own nest while inflicting pain lower down the hierarchy. Middle managers understand the need for the pain and are usually willing to accept it. However, the immunity or golden parachutes of those at the top is the source of considerable resentment. From the firm's perspective, this mistrust can have significant negative consequences. As one manager commented: "On Friday afternoon, you look around and you see how many people aren't here. You just wouldn't see that in the past. It's like people don't have the energy to get to Friday anymore. They are just getting out as soon as they can. And that's one way I've seen it. You just look around on a Friday afternoon, and it's different than it has been in the past . . . It's somewhat a loss of trust; it's somewhat, "We haven't got an increase; I want a life."

It is tempting to make the simple, and seemingly uncontroversial, assertion that the limited commitment of middle managers to the firm carries with it a cost that employers should seek to avoid. After all, logic holds that the extra effort and contribution of ideas required to be successful in today's hypercompetitive environment will not be forthcoming, given the widespread distrust felt by middle managers toward their superiors. While this assertion makes sense in principle, it might not hold in practice. Management scholars with good hearts write about firms, such as Southwest Airlines or SAS Institute, that prosper, seemingly because they treat their employees as an asset to be retained.[11] But these scholars tend to ignore counter-examples, such as General Electric, which have also prospered despite taking a much more transactional view of their workforce. Certainly, more firms are on the GE end of the spectrum than on the Southwest Airlines end, yet productivity and profits have done quite well in recent years.

The case for fairness is therefore not a slam-dunk, but it is nonetheless strong. In what James March and Herbert Simon call the "machine model" of organizations, employee attitudes are irrelevant; employees simply follow orders.[12] However, in reality, employee effort does depend upon people's affective commitment to the firm, and the managers with whom I spoke were clearly disaffected by the lack of fairness. They liked their work and took care in doing it—their craft attitudes—but the extent to which they were willing to go the extra mile was variable.

There are two distinct versions of the fairness discussion, one of which speaks to the individual behavior of senior executives and the other of which raises deeper questions about the purposes of the corporation. Neither are uncontroversial, but the former is certainly more likely to gain broad support.

Middle managers looking up often see (and resent) top executives giving themselves (either directly or via boards that are not at arm's-length) various financial rewards and cushions that are unavailable lower down the hierarchy. It would seem to be a basic principle of fairness that pain should be broadly shared. Moreover, firms would go a long way toward regaining the attachment of management (and other employees) were they to follow this simple principle.

Some of the rewards given to top management seem clearly over the top. Jack Welch of GE laid off thousands, but when he left, the board granted him, in addition to a generous deferred salary and pension, an apartment in Manhattan complete with food, wine, servants, and laundry service. The lifetime Red Sox tickets that Chad Gifford received upon selling Fleet to Bank of America is another example. Beyond these sorts of perks, which simply seem provocative, is the pattern that CEOs do not have an arm's-length relationship with their boards of directors and, in many respects, set their own pay.[13]

The deeper and much more difficult issue regarding fairness is the question of in whose interest the firm operates. Should the firm primarily seek to maximize the wealth of stock owners, or are there other constituencies, stakeholders, whose interests should also receive attention? Using the same language I used in the discussion of Bill Belichick's management style, is the only goal to win a Super Bowl and hence please the season ticket holders? Or, should the team be willing to accept some reduction in its chances in order to show some loyalty to longtime players who have built the franchise, or should it perhaps enhance the situation of other stakeholders? The answer might seem self-evident in the case of a football team, but it is not necessarily straightforward for a corporation. Firms have multiple constituencies, including stockholders, employees, the communities in which they operate, and the wider public. Are the interests of just one of these stakeholders paramount, or does the firm need to make some trade-offs? Ironically, before the financial-market revolution ratcheted up pressure on firms to maximize share prices, the CEOs of many American firms did in fact take a broader stakeholder perspective, sacrificing some profits for other goals. Whether this is desirable and just what the trade-offs should be remains an open question.

Stakeholder Perspectives

The conventional view, of course, is that corporations are the creature of their shareholders and do and should operate only in those shareholders' interests. Virtually all the middle managers I interviewed bought into this as a first reaction, although on reflection, some backed off a little. "This is business" was the most common comment. Many managers went a step further and argued that unless a firm behaved as it was doing and made profits the paramount objective, it would put all its employees at risk instead of just those who were laid off. There were, however, some variations on this theme.

"Roy," a back-office manager and two-time loser, illustrates this well. His first career was at Digital Equipment Corporation (DEC), the legendary computer firm founded by former MIT engineer Ken Olsen. DEC not only was a technology success, but was also widely viewed as a great place to work, the closest someone could come to a university setting in private industry. But DEC crashed and eventually disappeared, caught by the personal computer and open-architecture revolution and unable to adapt. Roy lost his job and went to Fleet. There he did well, rising to manage a reasonable-sized unit, but with the Bank of America merger, he was terminated. What are his views about to whom the firm has responsibility? "You know, corporations don't owe their employees anything. I mean, they paid me a fair wage. I was lucky enough to move up within the ranks while I could. [I] certainly enjoyed my tenure there, at both places. It's when you get forced down a path, those are the pieces that you can't control . . . I think people need to have a voice."

What starts off as a very standard perspective ends up with what appears to be a plea for greater employee involvement in decision making. Just what Roy means is far from clear, but there is, in fact, a debate among scholars of corporate governance about in whose interest the firm operates. Scholars and activists who view shifts in governance arrangements as a central strategy for improving outcomes experienced by employees make several different points, some of which are more threatening to the traditional conception of the role of the firm than others. The least threatening arguments focus on the particular institutional framework within which governance is conducted. One version accepts the centrality of stockholders, but argues that the institutional setup of financial markets leads to an excessive focus on short-term stock gains rather than maximizing value in the long run. The emphasis on the short term makes it difficult for the firm to undertake investments, such as those in people, that have a long payback period. This view does not fundamentally challenge the primacy of the stockholder, but rather claims that their interests are being poorly served by the current system and that improvements would also make employees better off. A deeper challenge contests the core belief that the only legitimate objective of the firm is to maximize stakeholder value.

In the eyes of most American economists, the stakeholder view is an invitation to economic inefficiency. Profits, distributed to stockholders, are essential signals of efficient allocation of capital. A stakeholder firm will be of the wrong size: if conditions indicate it should grow (due to increasing demand or technological dynamism), it will not attract enough capital, because some of the returns are diverted to others. If the firm should shrink because it is in a declining sector or because of excess capacity for its product, internal capital will be retained for too long in order to appease the various constituencies. More generally, by contaminating relative price signals, in this case the returns to capital, the economy as a whole will be less productive than it otherwise could be. It would be better, in this view, to follow the rules of economic efficiency and then use the gains to remedy whatever negative outcomes the political process identifies.

In an effort to more firmly ground the stakeholder view, Margaret Blair and Mark Roe have made related arguments.[14]

Blair points out that modern economic theory assigns owner-ship rights to shareholders on the grounds that they bear the residual risk of the enterprise. That is, employees and suppliers are paid according to a contract, whereas the owners only receive a return on their investment if something is left over. Because they bear this residual risk, the owners should have control, says the shareholder model. Both Blair and Roe argue, however, that in reality, employees bear a residual risk, because they have made specific investments in the firm, largely through learning skills, which only pay off over time and usually at a particular employer. Furthermore, economic efficiency clearly requires that invest-ments of this sort be encouraged. Thus, even if we ignore fair-ness concerns, there remain efficiency reasons why employees are legitimate stakeholders who should have a voice in gover-nance decisions.

This line of thinking has been endorsed by some very senior mainstream organizational economists, for example, Stanford's John Roberts and Paul Milgrom: "With high level of firm spe-cific human capital, the decisions taken by the firm place risks on employee's human assets that are comparable to those borne by investors in physical capital. Protecting the value of human capital then requires that employee's interests figure into the firm's decision making."[15]

In the normal course of events, one would expect that share-holders would be sensitive to these considerations because they too want to encourage employee investments in the firm. With this in mind, the firm would enter into explicit or implicit con-tracts to protect the investments of workers and suppliers, and reputational considerations (if these contracts were broken, the firm would not be able to attract workers or suppliers in the future) would be an effective enforcement mechanism. The problem, however, is that in an epoch of economic turbulence, there may come a point when a firm finds it worthwhile to break these commitments, even though the stakeholders would oppose such an action. In fact, one interpretation of takeovers is that they provide rationale for such a "breach of trust" via the actions of new owners, who bear none of the prior commitments of the old regime.[16]

Whether fairness considerations should extend to rethinking the ultimate responsibility of the firm is not an easy question. Certainly in today's environment, such an exercise does seem somewhat farfetched. Nevertheless, a wise firm, faced with the disaffection of its middle managers and the cynical views of its new hires, would probably do well to move more in the direction of fairness than has been typical. What's more, such a firm would also do well to protect the implicit investments of its employees.

CONCLUSION

We live in an era in which CEOs are glorified. It is not just that a "cult of the personality" has developed around leaders such as Jack Welch, but also the assumption that the key determinant of success in most organizations is the identity of the CEO. Newspaper stories about the success or failure of this or that firm consistently emphasize the identity and traits of top management. Boards of directors have bought into this. When a firm is doing badly or when there is a felt need to embark on new directions, the first instinct is to replace the managers at the top.

At the same time that the CEO is glorified, middle management is disparaged. The pop management literature is full of critical references to middle management. At a more practical level, consulting firms earn their daily bread by advising their clients to eviscerate managerial ranks.

It would be foolish to argue that the CEO is not relevant to organizational performance, and it would be equally foolish to claim that no firm should ever reduce its managerial ranks. But the fundamental spirit of the times is wrong. As a group, middle managers are central, indeed crucial, to an organization's success. Middle managers perform much of the day-to-day work of the organization, but beyond this, they are much like general managers in that they are responsible for making many of the judgment calls and trade-offs that shape the firm's success. They are also the key communications channel from senior management down through the ranks. They are committed to their work and, with their craft orientation, strive to perform at a high level.

If management gurus have erred in bashing middle management, so have social scientists erred in dismissing managers as victimized drones or, at the other extreme, as a group ripe to respond politically to their travails. Middle managers are well aware that their circumstances have shifted and that their hold on their jobs is more tenuous than in the past. They are much more skeptical of top management than they were before and in some respects are alienated from their organizations. But these people are committed to their work and gain considerable satisfaction from it. The spread of ad hoc and project teams has given many of them more variety and autonomy than they had experienced in the past. Middle managers are increasingly arriving at a sensible balance of work and private life, and they are articulate in explaining these choices and in drawing boundaries.

Both organizations and social scientists need to revise their views of middle managers. Middle management has oscillated from being invisible to being a target. Both perspectives are wrong. Middle managers should be valued for what they contribute and should be seen as a resource to be developed. Such a perspective is more accurate and healthier and would be more productive for all concerned.

NOTES

Chapter 1

1. There are, of course, some exceptions. For example, Vicki Smith, *Managing in the Corporate Interest: Control and Resistance in an American Bank* (Berkeley: University of California Press, 1990), conducted interviews at a bank that later became part of the bank examined in this book. In her interviews, she studied how the bank's middle managers responded to restructuring.

2. Ibid., 14.

3. Quoted in Gideon Kunda and Galit Ailon-Souday, "Managers, Markets, and Ideologies: Design and Devotion Revisited," in *The Oxford Handbook on Work and Organization*, ed. Stephen Ackroyd et al. (New York: Oxford, 2005), p. 204.

4. Quoted in David Gordon, *Fat and Mean: The Corporate Squeeze of Working Americans and the Myth of Managerial "Downsizing"* (New York: Free Press, 1996), 50–51.

5. A detailed discussion of the sources of these data and definitions is provided in chapter 3, in the text and the notes.

6. C. Wright Mills, *White Collar: The American Middle Class* (New York: Oxford University Press, 1956), 80.

7. Marianne Bertrand and Antoinette Schoar, "Managing with Style: The Effect of Managers on Firm Policies," *Quarterly Journal of Economics* 118, no. 4 (November 2003): 1169–1208.

8. Whenever only the first name of a person is used in this book, it is a fictitious name used to protect the person's privacy.

Chapter 2

1. Alfred D. Chandler, *The Visible Hand* (Cambridge, MA: Belknap Press, 1977), 459.

2. Ibid., 463.

3. Reinhard Bendix, *Work and Authority in Industry* (Berkeley, CA: University of California Press, 1956), 221.

4. Mauro Guillen, *Models of Management: Work, Authority, and Organization in Comparative Perspective* (Chicago: University of Chicago Press, 1994), 308.

5. Chandler, *The Visible Hand*, 411.

6. Peter Cappelli, *Talent on Demand: Managing Talent in an Age of Uncertainty* (Boston: Harvard Business School Press, 2008).

7. See Douglas W. Bray, Richard J. Campbell, and Donald L. Grant, *Formative Years in Business: A Long-Term AT&T Study of Managerial Lives* (New York: Wiley, 1974).

8. George Baker, Michael Gibbs, and Bengt Holmstrom, "The Internal Economics of the Firm: Evidence from Personnel Data," *Quarterly Journal of Economics* 109, no. 4 (November 1994): 881–919.

9. John-Paul MacDuffie, "Automotive White-Collar: The Changing Status and Roles of Salaried Employees in the North American Automobile Industry," in *Broken Ladders: Managerial Careers in the New Economy*, ed. Paul Osterman (New York: Oxford University Press, 1996), 97.

10. David Gordon, *Fat and Mean: The Corporate Squeeze of Working Americans and the Myth of Managerial "Downsizing"* (New York: Free Press, 1996), 47.

11. Michael Hammer and James Champy, *Reengineering the Corporation* (New York: HarperCollins, 1993), 41–43.

12. Ibid., 78, 208.

13. See, for example, Quy Nguyen Huy, "In Praise of Middle Managers," *Harvard Business Review*, September 2001, 72–79.

14. D. Quinn Mills and G. Bruce Friesen, *Broken Promises: An Unconventional View of What Went Wrong at IBM* (Boston: Harvard Business School Press, 1996), 13.

15. Quoted in ibid., 67.

16. Louis Gerstner, *Who Says Elephants Can't Dance? Inside IBM's Historic Turnaround* (New York: HarperCollins, 2002), 64, 192, 194.

17. Ibid., p. 208.

18. "IBM to Change Pension Benefits," *New York Times*, May 4, 1999.

19. "Verizon to Cut Manager Pensions," *Wall Street Journal*, December 6, 2005.

20. Steve Lohr, "How Is the Game Played Now?" *New York Times*, December 5, 2005.

21. Steve Lohr, "IBM Plan Ties Training and Accounts," *New York Times*, July 25, 2007.

22. Quoted in "Speaking Out: IBM's Sam Palmisano," Business-Week Online, August 25, 2003, http://www.businessweek.com/magazine/content/03_34/b3846636.htm; and in "Hungry Tiger, Dancing Elephant: How Globalization Is Changing IBM's World," *The Economist*, April 7–13, 2007, 67.

23. C. Wright Mills, *White Collar: The American Middle Class* (New York: Oxford University Press, 1956), xii, 87, 107.

24. William H. Whyte, *The Organization Man* (New York: Doubleday, 1956), 3.

25. Louis Uchitelle and Nick Kleinfield, "On the Battlefields of Business, Millions of Casualties," *New York Times*, March 3, 1996.

26. Rick Bragg, "Big Holes Where the Dignity Used to Be," *New York Times*, March 5, 1996.

27. Richard Sennett, *The Corrosion of Character: The Personal Consequences of Work in the New Capitalism* (New York: W. W. Norton, 1998), 24, 30–31, 147.

28. The term *post entrepreneurial workplace* is from Rosabeth Moss Kanter, *When Giants Learn to Dance: Mastering the Challenge of Strategy, Management, and Careers in the 1990s* (New York: Simon and Schuster, 1989). The term *boundaryless career* is from Michael Arthur and Denise Rousseau, eds., *The Boundaryless Career* (New York: Oxford University Press, 1996).

29. Raymond Miles and Charles Snow, "Twenty-First Century Careers," in *The Boundaryless Career*, ed. Michael Arthur and Denise Rousseau (New York: Oxford University Press, 1996), p. 106.

30. Kanter, *When Giants Learn to Dance*, 299.

31. Quoted in Gideon Kunda and Galit Ailon-Souday, "Managers, Markets, and Ideologies: Design and Devotion Revisited," in *The Oxford Handbook on Work and Organization*, ed. Stephen Ackroyd et al. (New York: Oxford, 2005), 205.

Chapter 3

1. U.S. Bureau of Labor Statistics, "Employer Costs for Employee Compensation, March, 2007," USLD-7-0877, available at http://stats.bls.gov/news.release/archives/ecec_06212007.pdf.

2. Ibid. This figure is for "management, business, and financial operations occupations."

3. "Severance Packages Grow More Generous," *Wall Street Journal*, December 7, 2005.

4. The source for the dislocation figures is U.S. Bureau of Labor Statistics, "Worker Displacement, 2001–2003," news release dated July 30, 2004. The source for total employment by occupation is U.S. Bureau of Labor Statistics, www.bls.gov/emp.

5. Paul Osterman, *Securing Prosperity: How the American Labor Market Has Changed and What to Do about It* (Princeton, NJ: Princeton University Press, 1998), 29.

6. Kevin Hallock, "A Descriptive Analysis of Layoffs in Large U.S. Firms Using Archival Data Over Three Decades and Interviews with Senior Managers," working paper, Cornell Industrial and Labor Relations School, Ithaca, NY, August 2005.

7. This is the definition of managers used, for example, by Glenn R. Carroll and Albert C. Teo, "On the Social Network of Managers," *Academy of Management Journal* 39, no. 2 (April 1996): 421–440.

8. As I work with the surveys, I will present data only on managers who have a college degree or more, because in the job-tenure surveys, there are no data on whether people are paid on an hourly or salaried basis. I use *college* as a proxy for *salaried*, and this has an additional virtue that managers in larger firms are substantially more likely to have college degrees than are managers in small enterprises. Hence, a college degree is a reasonable proxy for a salaried employee. The census surveys that ask about job tenure do not, unfortunately, also ask about firm size. But other monthly census surveys do collect this information, and there is a reasonably strong relationship between the education level of managers and the size of the firms in which they work. For example, in March 2006 among managers who worked in firms of one thousand or more employees, 61 percent had a college degree, whereas among managers in firms of ten to twenty-four employees, only 43 percent had a degree.

9. There is one important qualification: As already noted, in 2002, the occupational classification changed. As a result, the definition of managers is somewhat different in 2006 from what it was earlier. It is possible to estimate the degree of overlap; about 80 percent of the people who were classified as managers in 2006 would have been classified as managers in the earlier years. These estimates of overlap are based on analysis of the 2002 National Bureau of Economic Research May Current Population Survey files. The analysis includes both the old and the new occupational classifications. There is enough change, however, that considerable caution should be used. We can nevertheless have much more confidence in what the data show

regarding shifts from 1987 to 2000, a period that encompasses what is popularly seen as the era in which managerial work was transformed.

10. Bond, Galinsky, and Swanberg, *The 1997 National Study of the Changing Workforce* (New York: Families and Work Institute, 1998).

Chapter 4

1. Chester Barnard, *The Functions of the Executive* (Cambridge: Harvard University Press, 1938), p. 217.

2. Melville Dalton, *Men Who Manage* (New York: Wiley, 1959), p. 265.

3. Quoted in Henry Mintzberg, *The Nature of Managerial Work* (New York: Harper & Row, 1973), 57.

4. Mintzberg, *The Nature of Managerial Work*, 171.

5. Richard Hackman, *Leading Teams: Setting the Stage for Great Performance* (Boston: Harvard Business School Press, 2002).

6. John Kotter, *The General Managers* (New York: Free Press, 1982).

7. James Womack and Daniel Roos, *The Machine That Changed the World: The Story of Lean Production—Toyota's Secret Weapon in the Global Car Wars That Is Revolutionizing World Industry* (New York: Free Press, 2007); Frank Levy and Richard Murnane, *Teaching the New Basic Skills: Principles for Educating Children to Thrive in a Changing Economy* (New York: Free Press, 1996).

8. For a useful discussion of this issue and extensive references, see National Research Council, *Research on Future Skill Demands: A Workshop Summary* (Washington, DC: National Academies Press), 2008.

9. Douglas Bray, Richard Campbell, and Donald Grant, *Formative Years in Business: A Long-Term AT&T Study of Managerial Lives* (New York: Wiley, 1974).

10. David Granick, *Managerial Comparisons in Four Developed Countries: France, Britain, the United States, and Russia* (Cambridge, MA: MIT Press, 1972), 218.

11. Harland Prechel, "Economic Crisis and the Centralization of Control over the Managerial Process: Corporate Restructuring and Neo-Fordist Decision-Making," *American Sociological Review* 59, no. 5 (October 1994): 723–745.

Chapter 5

1. Rosabeth Moss Kanter, *Men and Women of the Corporation* (New York: Basic Books, 1993).

2. Robert Jackell, *Moral Mazes* (New York: Oxford University Press, 1988), 43.

3. Ibid., 33.

4. Ibid., 44 and 75.

5. Douglas Bray, Richard Campbell, and Donald Grant, *Formative Years in Business: A Long-Term AT&T Study of Managerial Lives* (New York: Wiley, 1974), 179; and Kanter, *Men and Women*, 140.

6. Muriel Niederle and Lise Vesterlund, "Do Women Shy Away from Competition? Do Men Compete Too Much?" *Quarterly Journal of Economics* 122, no. 3 (August 2007): 1067–1102.

7. Peter Cappelli, *Talent on Demand: Managing Talent in an Age of Uncertainty* (Boston: Harvard Business School Press, 2008), 61.

8. James Medoff and Katherine Abraham, "Experience, Performance, and Earnings," *Quarterly Journal of Economics* 95, no. 4 (December 1980): 703–736.

9. Wayne Casico and Herman Aguinis, *Applied Psychology in Human Resource Management*, 6th ed. (New York: Prentice Hall, 2004), 64.

10. Jackell, *Moral Mazes*, 193.

11. Linda Babcock et al., "Nice Girls Don't Ask," *Harvard Business Review*, October 2003, 14–16.

12. Alice H. Eagly and Steven J. Karau, "Role Congruity Theory of Prejudice Towards Female Leaders," *Psychological Review* 109, no. 3 (2002): 584.

13. Larry W. Hunter et al., "It's Not Just the ATMs: Firm Strategies, Work Restructuring, and Workers' Earnings in Retail Banking," *Industrial and Labor Relations Review* 54, no. 2A (2001): 402–424.

14. Raghuram Rajan and Julie Wulf, "The Flattening Firm: Evidence from Panel Data on the Changing Nature of Corporate Hierarchies," working paper 9633, Cambridge, MA: National Bureau of Economic Research, April 2003.

Chapter 6

1. C. Wright Mills, *White Collar: The American Middle Class* (New York: Oxford University Press, 1956), xvi.

2. Randy Hodson, "Dignity in the Workplace Under Participative Management: Alienation and Freedom Revisited," *American Sociological Review* 61 (October 1996).

3. Quote from Robert Jackell, *Moral Mazes* (New York: Oxford University Press, 1988), 75.

4. Quote from Chester Barnard, *The Functions of the Executive* (Cambridge: Harvard University Press, 1938), 144.

5. William H. Whyte, *The Organization Man* (New York: Doubleday, 1956), 4.

6. Ibid., p. 143.

7. Douglas Bray, Richard Campbell, and Donald Grant, *Formative Years in Business: A Long-Term AT&T Study of Managerial Lives* (New York: Wiley, 1974), 154, 177.

8. Vicki Smith, *Managing in the Corporate Interest: Control and Resistance in an American Bank* (Berkeley: University of California Press, 1990).

9. http://pewresearch.org/pubs/318/american-work-life-is-worsening-but-most-workers-still-content.

10. Gretchen Morgenstern, "Fair Game: A Year to Suspend Disbelief," *New York Times*, December 31, 2006.

11. Eric Dash, "Gilded Paychecks/Possible Solutions: Compensation Experts Offer Ways to Help Curb Executive Salaries," *New York Times*, December 30, 2006.

12. In the Standard & Poor's 500, average CEO pay exploded from $3.2 million in 1992 to $14.7 million in 2000 (Brian Hall and Kevin Murphy, "The Trouble with Stock Options," *Journal of Economic Perspectives* 17, no. 3 [2003]: 51). Hall and Murphy say the average CEO in the Standard & Poor's 500 made 30 times what the average production worker received in pay. By 2002, cash compensation for CEOs was 90 times that of the average production worker, and total compensation was 360 times workers' compensation (ibid.: 63). Carola Frydman and Raven Saks, "Historical Trends in Executive Compensation," working paper, MIT Sloan School of Management, Cambridge, MA, 2005, have studied a longer time series, 1936–2005, sampling two hundred to three hundred of the largest firms over this period. The study includes the value of all compensation (base pay, performance bonuses, and stock options) and finds that CEO wages relative to those of the average production worker saw a contraction in 1940–1970 and then widened to a ratio of 110 to 1, twice the ratio prior to World War II.

13. Jim Rutenberg, "Bush Tells Wall St. to Rethink Pay Practices," *New York Times*, February 1, 2007.

14. Lars Osberg and Timothy Smeeding, "'Fair' Inequality? An International Comparison of Attitudes to Pay Differentials," working paper, Maxwell School, Syracuse University, June 2005.

15. Shasa Talcott, "Gifford's Friends Will Fly For Free," *Boston Globe*, January 27, 2005, C1.

16. See the description in Jackell, *Moral Mazes*, p. 25.

17. Raghuram Rajan and Julie Wulf, "The Flattening Firm: Evidence from Panel Data on the Changing Nature of Corporate Hierarchies," working paper 9633, Cambridge, MA: National Bureau of Economic Research, April 2003.

18. Larry W. Hunter et al., "It's Not Just the ATMs: Firm Strategies, Work Restructuring, and Workers' Earnings in Retail Banking," *Industrial and Labor Relations Review* 54, no. 2A (2001): 402–424.

19. Michael Jensen and Kevin Murphy, "Remuneration: Where We Have Been, How We Got Here, What Are the Problems, and How to Fix Them," finance working paper 44/2004, Brussels, European Corporate Governance Institute, July 2004.

20. Frydman and Saks, "Executive Compensation"; see also Rakesh Khurana, *In Search of the Corporate Savior: The Irrational Quest for Charismatic CEOs* (Princeton, NJ: Princeton University Press, 2002), p. 197.

21. Charles C. Heckscher, *White-Collar Blues: Management Loyalties in an Age of Corporate Restructuring* (New York: Basic Books, 1995).

22. Sanford Jacoby, ed., *Masters to Managers: Historical and Comparative Perspectives on American Employers* (New York: Columbia University Press, 1991), p. 176.

23. The survey was sent to members of graduating classes of 2000 and 2005. The overall response rate was 39 percent, which produced 308 usable responses. There were no demographic correlates to the response rate, but the students who responded had a slightly higher grade point average than those who did not.

24. The total in the table sums to 103 instead of 100 because a few respondents exceeded the 100-point limit.

Chapter 7

1. Ely Chinoy, *Automobile Workers and the American Dream* (Garden City, NJ: Doubleday, 1955).

2. William H. Whyte, *The Organization Man* (New York: Doubleday, 1956), p. 101.

3. Peter Drucker, *The Practice of Management* (New York: Perennial Library, 1954), 122–123.

4. Charles C. Heckscher, *White-Collar Blues: Management Loyalties in an Age of Corporate Restructuring* (New York: Basic Books, 1995), p. 151.

5. These numbers are based on my calculations using data from U.S. Census Bureau, "Current Population Survey," Tenure Supplement, January 2006. See chapter 3 for a more detailed methodological discussion.

6. Forrest Briscoe and Matthew Bidwell, "Who Contracts? Determinants of Decisions to Work As Independent Contractors Among Information Technology Professionals," working paper, Penn State University, State College, PA, August 2006.

7. Andrew Abbott, *The System of Professions* (Chicago: University of Chicago Press, 1988).

8. Ibid., 9.

9. This point is made in Rakesh Khurana, *From Higher Aims to Hired Hands: The Social Transformation of American Business Schools and the Unfulfilled Promise of Management as a Profession* (Princeton, NJ: Princeton University Press, 2007).

10. For a discussion of these ideas, see Paul Osterman et al., *Working in America* (Cambridge, MA: MIT Press, 2001).

11. See, for example, Jeffrey Pfeffer, *Competitive Advantage Through People* (Boston: Harvard Business School Press, 1996).

12. James March and Herbert Simon, *Organizations* (New York: Wiley, 1958), 37.

13. For additional evidence on this, see Lucian Bebchuk and Jesse Fried, *Pay Without Performance: The Unfilled Promise of Executive Compensation* (Cambridge, MA: Harvard University Press, 2004).

14. Margaret Blair, *Ownership and Control: Rethinking Corporate Governance for the Twenty-first Century* (Washington: Brookings Institution, 1995), chapter 7; Mark Roe, *Strong Managers, Weak Owners* (Princeton, NJ: Princeton University Press, 1996), 261.

15. Paul Milgrom and John Roberts, *Economics, Organization, and Management* (New York: Prentice Hall, 1992), 351.

16. Andrei Shleifer and Lawrence Summers, "Breach of Trust in Hostile Takeovers," *NBER Working Paper Series* 2342 (May 1989).

INDEX

ABOUT THE AUTHOR

Paul Osterman is the Nanyang Technological University (NTU) Professor of Human Resources and Management at the Massachusetts Institute of Technology Sloan School of Management. He served four years as deputy dean at the Sloan School and two years as head of the Department of Behavioral and Policy Sciences.

Osterman has served on several committees of the National Academy of Sciences and is a member of the board of directors of Jobs for the Future. Among other activities, he is coeditor of the *International Labor Review,* has been a panel member for the American Assembly, served on the research advisory panel of the W.E. Upjohn Institute for Employment Research, and has spoken widely to business, nonprofit, and government groups.

The Truth About Middle Managers is Osterman's tenth book. Among his most recent other books are *Securing Prosperity: How the American Labor Market Has Changed and What to Do About It* (Princeton, NJ: Princeton University Press, 1998) and *Working in America: A Blueprint for the New Labor Market* (Cambridge, MA: MIT Press, 2001).

DATE DUE